Praise for Ruth Poundwh

Quietly Ambitious Ph

"Ruth's philosophy has stopped me hiding from the hard stuff, and opened me up to my REAL self which I now realise was being stifled by all sorts of unhelpful noise, pressure and expectations."

—Tamsin Williamson, Life and Mindset Coach

"Knowing that I can be ambitious in my own way; in a slow, gentle, conscious way, that doesn't cast aside my values, has allowed me to build my business in a way that truly supports me."

—Alana Holloway, Chronic Illness Coach

"Ruth and the information she shares is a breath of fresh air in the online business space. I've never felt so validated and supported as I do when I *finally* hear someone endorsing finding ways to run a business that suit you."

—Vanessa Smith, Systems Strategist and Creative

"Everything that Ruth embodies has given me permission to be entirely myself in all areas of my life, not just my coaching business."

—Sarah Lynas, Self-Belief Coach

"We need more Ruths to show us that you can show up and contribute in your own way (the only way for it to be sustainable!)"

—Li-Yeng Choo

"I can deeply relate to being 'Quietly Ambitious'. Ruth has changed the way I look at being a business owner, and she continues to be an inspiration for how I want to map out the future of my business."

—Samantha Downes, Virtual Assistant

"It helped me to increase my trust in myself and the work I do, knowing I can be of service to my people without being someone else."

—Lavinia Basso, Life & Job Coach

"So many insights about myself as a business owner, but most importantly as a human."

—Anouk B Godbout, Parent Photographer and Mentor

"Ruth's work is a breath of fresh air, a reminder to focus on what matters most: authenticity & connection to yourself as a human being."

—Ava Gao, Empowered Parent Coach at *The Curious Mama*

"I wanted to be successful, I knew I felt ambitious, but I also knew I wanted to put my purpose, feelings and overall wellbeing at the heart of my business. So Ruth's philosophy has really been life-changing."

—Katy Pearson, Internal Communications Consultant for small and growing businesses and charities at *In A Word – Awesome*

"It has helped me believe it is possible to run my business in a way that works for me, not what works for someone else... to play to MY strengths, not what I think my strengths should be."

—Rachael Chrystal, Coach and GP

"You have such a beautiful way of being vulnerable and still make me want to work with you. You have created space and energy that allows people to feel comfortable doing the same! (showing up as my true, authentic, sensitive, softy self)"
—Alex Waggoner, Freelance Writer & Copy Coach

"I felt empowered to run things in a way that aligned with my own personality, and ultimately I feel much happier in my work."
—Erica Paton, Artist

"...a solid affirmation that as an introvert I can make up the rules of how I show up, that I can create offers that align with how I want to use my energy, and that I can also create space to rest within this work. (You also have the best journaling prompts I've ever used!)"
—Katrina Wolff, Soilpreneur

"Contorting myself into the stereotype shape of an entrepreneur is not sustainable long term. But being a quietly ambitious human is!"
—Fiona Thomas, Author, *Out of Office: Ditch the 9-5 and Be Your Own Boss*

Quietly Ambitious

How to Show Up in Your Online Business as a Sensitive and Heart-Led Introvert

Ruth Poundwhite

Quietly Ambitious Publishing

PUBLISHED BY RUTH POUNDWHITE

RUTHPOUNDWHITE.COM

Copyright © 2022 by Ruth Poundwhite

Book doula services and book design by Genevieve Parker Hill

Cover background design by Hira Sameer Ahmed

(hirasahmed.com)

All rights reserved. No part of this book may be reproduced or used in any manner without the prior written permission of the copyright owner, except for the use of brief quotations in a book review.

*For exclusive bonuses & resources to support you with owning your quiet ambition, visit **ruthpoundwhite.com/bookbonus***

For Rowan, who was the catalyst for everything I'm about to share, for Chris, who always inspires me to be a better version of myself, & for past me, who was so much braver than I gave her credit for.

CONTENTS

Preface 1

Introduction: My First Decade in Online Business 3

Chapter 1: On Feeling Good In Business, Making My Own Rules, and Ignoring the Noise 11

Chapter 2: On Being A Highly Sensitive Introvert in Online Business 17

Chapter 3: The Soulful, Simple, and Effective Way to Do Email Marketing 31

Chapter 4: 5 Things I Would Tell the Summer 2018 Version of Me 51

Chapter 5: On Making Mistakes & Learning The Right Lessons .. 61

Chapter 6: On Being Visible, Honest, and Always Scared 71

Chapter 7: Journalling for Business Owners 83

Chapter 8: How to Keep Showing Up (Even When It's Hard) 99

Chapter 9: Our Businesses Can Change the World 113

Chapter 10: Are You Allowing Yourself Support? 133

Chapter 11: Honouring Our Natural Cycles Of Creation (& Prioritising Rest) 145

Chapter 12: How I Do It All (& The Power of Imperfect Experimentation) 159

Chapter 13: Identifying Your Unique Glass Ceiling of Possibility 167

Afterword 175
Acknowledgements 177
About The Author 179

PREFACE

I'm an ambitious woman.

While I'm happy to use that word now, it didn't feel right for a long time.

When I started my business, all I saw were loud, shiny marketers—and that's not who I was or who I aimed to be. Based on what those loud, shiny marketers were telling me, I thought ambition had to mean sacrifice, hustle, and doing it "the right way".

I thought this meant I wasn't ambitious because my business goals didn't look how I thought they "should". But just because I was introverted, sensitive, and didn't shout about my goals, it didn't mean that I wasn't incredibly driven to make things happen in my life, to make an impact with my work, and to make good money doing it.

So I decided to own this side of myself, and I called it "quietly ambitious."

Quietly ambitious is still "ambitious" at its core, but it's a version of ambitious that lets you more fully embrace *your own* internally-driven version of success. It's simply a steppingstone to unconditionally owning and loving who you are and what *you* want to create in your life and business.

INTRODUCTION: MY FIRST DECADE IN ONLINE BUSINESS

I've been working for myself for over 10 years now.

My online business journey started in 2008. I had graduated from university, it was the time of the credit crunch, and I didn't know what I wanted to do (and my Philosophy and History degree didn't exactly help me get a job).

I applied to do a Master's in museum studies as a way to avoid figuring out what I really wanted. Which wasn't a great reason to do a Master's, so I dropped out at the last minute and started looking for a job – any job! But the recession (and, honestly, my distinct lack of enthusiasm) meant I was turned down for almost everything.

Someone suggested I might make some money proofreading and, in my search to find out more, I discovered an entire new world of online marketing. Business owners were looking for writers in a huge variety of niches. So I replied to a job ad on a forum, wrote an article about ethical travel, and received the payment in my PayPal account that same day. It blew my mind!

I kept applying for writing jobs, and it was easy to find work (this was a time when website owners would fill sites with informational content to make money from Google Ads). Some of the work was interesting. Some of it was far less interesting, but I generally enjoyed having the opportunity to research a huge range of topics, from haunted pubs around the UK to vegetarianism.

Before then, my experience of writing online came from my (anonymous) blog. I loved exploring myself and the world as I saw it through this blog. But the paid writing wasn't the same. It wasn't about giving myself time and space to understand and explore the world – it became a question of how many words I could pack into a day, and it soon became exhausting.

I quickly earned a "full-time income" (as in, I matched the minimum wage I used to earn in retail), but I was working myself into the ground. It was a good way to make money while I didn't have a job, but I charged a pittance. So that "full-time income" came about as a result of writing like a machine. It wasn't sustainable, and I burned myself out.

Writing quickly lost its magic, and I had learned a lot from my clients (and from my own blog), so I took a break. I put together some ready-made packages of content, and small ready-to-go websites with a bank of content to get them going and "flipped" them. It was fun: I was in control of the topics, and the money was much better.

In 2010 (two years into my business) I read *The 4-Hour Workweek* by Tim Ferriss. While the book is far from perfect – the philosophy suggests that success is down to our individual willingness to "do the work", failing to acknowledge the broader systems we operate under – it opened my mind to a completely new way of living. I had been so focused on working hard and making "just enough" money that I didn't realise the privileged position I had found myself in: running an online business that I could travel with, and the possibility of scaling that business by hiring others. And that's what I did.

The seed had been planted, and my then-boyfriend (now husband) had just finished his Master's degree while working part time, so it was the perfect time to think seriously about travelling long term. We didn't have much in the way of savings, but the plan was to keep earning through my business as we went. And as soon as that plan was in motion, I started to make more money.

We left for Bangkok on New Year's Eve, 2011, and spent the whole of 2012 slowly travelling and working through Thailand, Laos, Cambodia, Vietnam, Myanmar, Malaysia and Japan. We spent £14,000 between us that year, far less than we would have if we had stayed home.

The lower cost of living was a huge privilege, allowing my husband to quit his job and me to explore running my business in new ways with less pressure to earn what I would have needed to earn in the UK. After a few months of balancing the sightseeing, planning, and experiencing the travel alongside the work, I decided it was time to hire more support.

That year was my first taste of really designing my business around the life I wanted to live, and seeing on paper what a positive impact that could have on the numbers. And the year that followed – back in the UK, lacking in motivation, losing momentum and not knowing what was next – taught me how important it is for me to be working towards a goal (it's also a good reminder that business growth is rarely ever linear).

Things picked up again for me in my business when we got engaged, and I had a wedding to pay for. A switch had been flicked. I had a goal again, I went all in on my business, and it grew beyond what I had ever thought possible. We bought a house – something I had previously thought was impossible for us – and my team of writers got bigger and bigger. The business was growing year on year and I personally took on a more creative and managerial role.

In the space of three years I had drastically reduced my working hours and seen first-hand what a difference that (plus delegation) could make to my income. I was gradually shifting my mindset around what I thought nurturing a successful business had to look like, and who I thought I needed to be to do that.

My next big business lessons came, surprisingly, when I decided to run a marathon. Training involved frequent and long morning training runs. I was not fast; later runs could take three or more hours. And I took my time getting ready and recovering after each run, most weekdays. There was something magical about how *slow* it all was. I was nurturing my body, quieting my mind, and learning *how much more* flexible my schedule got to be. My income continued to grow, my workload didn't.

The growth was incredible, but with the increase in income came an increase in tax that I hadn't prepared for. I was spending money out of my business like it was *all* mine. I didn't separate my personal and business accounts, and I wasn't setting aside enough money for tax. By the end of 2016, I looked at the mess I had made, and I decided to do something about it. I was terrified of getting an accountant, I was terrified of how much tax I thought I owed, but I knew what needed to be done.

My biggest fear was that they would tell me I was doing it all wrong (which, by the way, is a very clear sign that you *need* an accountant in the first place). And my second-biggest fear was that I wouldn't be able to find an accountant who "got it" – who would understand the online business world, multiple currencies, EU VAT requirements and so on.

You'll hear me talk about trusting my gut throughout this book, but that was not something I felt comfortable doing back in 2016. Nevertheless, I came across an accountant online that I just *felt good* about, and it turned out to be the best decision I'd ever made in my business.

My new accountant helped me set up a limited company (a big but sometimes scary business milestone). We worked out salaries, dividends, and I began setting aside tax money as I earned it. It felt amazing to finally pay off my big tax bill and to know that I was never going to get in that situation again.

Which brings us to 2017. At this point I was pregnant with my son and growing increasingly dissatisfied with my business. I had the money and the house covered, which gave me the mental space to think about my higher needs: personal satisfaction and work *enjoyment*. I knew I wanted to do something else, but I was too scared to actually make it happen.

Meanwhile, planning for my maternity leave led to another huge uplevel in my business. I wasn't personally doing any of the day-to-day work of the business at this point. I hired a new assistant, I hired new writers, and I personally had to fit double the "bigger picture" and project management work in for a few months so that I could take five months off when I had my baby. I made it happen.

In those early years, my important mindset shifts were:

1. Having very specific life goals, like paying for my wedding, buying my home, and training for a marathon.

2. Treating my business more like a real business, hiring an accountant and setting aside money for taxes.
3. Learning to trust in who I was (instead of thinking I had to fight against it to be successful).

And then everything changed.

My beautiful son Rowan was born at the end of 2017. It was very hard, it was messy, it was also deeply empowering and a catalyst for huge changes in my life and work. It was the beginning of a new journey into *deep* self-trust.

In 2018 I launched my new website, RuthPoundwhite.com, to support other sensitive but ambitious humans to run a business in a way that works for them, just as I had figured out how to do over the last decade. Throughout this book I'll share more about what it took to get visible and to do the work that was always in my heart.

Those first ten years in online business took me from freshly graduated and clueless to discovering a whole new world and, eventually, building a business that served clients all around the world. And that work taught me so much about streamlining, running a simpler business, working less, earning more money, and figuring out the work that brought me joy.

Most importantly, I learned that I really could do this my way. Imperfectly and in all my sensitive and introverted glory.

I am so grateful to that first business for helping me to create the life I always wanted. I am completely unemployable at this point, and I wouldn't have it any other way.

In 2020, after running two businesses side by side for 18 months, I finally and fully quit my writing business to go "full-time" coaching other sensitive, introverted business owners to grow thriving online businesses, own their ambitions and step into visibility in a healthy way.

They say that *still waters run deep,* and that couldn't be more true of the humans I work with. They have a deep desire to serve, to make a positive difference to their corner of the world, and to get well paid for the work they love to do. They want to achieve all this in a way that is true to their heart-led, sensitive, introverted personalities. I'm proof that this (and so much more) is possible.

As you read this book, imagine we're sitting together chatting in a cosy café. We're talking and sharing notes on a new, anti-hustle way to run a thriving online business — with sensitivity, heart, honesty, self-love and -trust, ambition, courage, and plenty of rest. This book is my side of the conversation. I'll be sharing my thoughts about this quietly revolutionary way of doing business. My methods have worked for me, and they may work for you, but remember that there is no one, single "right way" of doing business.

I'd love to hear your side of the conversation. If any of the ideas in this book inspire you to reach out, please do so. You can get in touch through my website, RuthPoundwhite.com, or send me a message on Instagram @ruthpoundwhite.

CHAPTER 1: ON FEELING GOOD IN BUSINESS, MAKING MY OWN RULES, AND IGNORING THE NOISE

I started my first business when I couldn't get a job.

The way I started was not intentional – in fact, it was almost entirely accidental. As you know, I was looking for a way to make some money out of university and found out that I could do some freelance writing online. My "business" (which I would *never* have called a "business" back then) took its own course without me deciding exactly where I wanted it to go. I kept writing, I kept learning and I kept going, and at some point I eventually realised just how much potential this "business" had.

I believed a business was something that you grow, and to grow your business, you do X, Y, and Z. You do what the experts say you do. You work as hard as possible, you grow the numbers, you get more money, and then you go for a version of success that everyone talks about. The problem with this was that there was a very key ingredient missing: *how I personally felt about what I was doing*.

I believe that what people "feel" about what they're doing matters more for some than it does for others. I'm sure there are people out there who can run a successful business without feeling that it needs to reflect their personal values or feel exactly "like them". And I don't think there's anything wrong with being motivated purely by the money and the thrill of building and running a business. But I am not one of those people.

It has never worked for me to simply build a business for its own sake, and I have never been able to detach my feelings from the process (hello, sensitive empath/ INFJ – I'll talk about the role of personality more in Chapter 2). I regularly step back to consider my values, my strengths, my weaknesses, my needs, my capacity, my time, and how I feel about the work that I'm doing. And I wish I had stepped back to consider how to mould and shape my business around those considerations a lot sooner.

What suits me personally could be completely different to what suits you, and that's why, as a coach and mentor, I don't buy into "the rules" of online business.

What do I mean by "the rules"? It's what we've been brought up to believe about work and success. It's the way people try to sell you their blueprint, the way they shame you for doing it "wrong", or blame you when you don't do it their way. It's what can often leave you feeling *not good enough*. And *not good enough* is how I felt for a long time.

In the early days of my business, I judged myself against the hyper-productive, the hustlers and the "bro-marketers". It seemed that they were all about the outrageously luxurious lifestyle and "working harder in a year than most do in a lifetime" while sipping cocktails on the beach and fast cars, and, and, and… At least, this was the kind of marketing I was seeing from online business "experts" back in 2008.

At best it spoke to an extremely narrow version of success, and at worst it played off my fear and insecurity, leaving me believing I was doing something wrong. Step-by-step blueprints can be helpful, but only if they are tailored to who you are. There is no one-size-fits-all way of doing business. Ask me how I know...

In the early days, I spent a lot of time and money looking for the Magic Blueprint™. Each time I signed up for the next shiny course - and I did this for a long while after my business was growing and doing well financially – I was sending a message to myself that how I felt didn't matter. Worse, that how I felt needed to change.

I still love signing up to a new shiny course, but I no longer do it out of a feeling of not-good-enough-ness. So, what changed? How did I turn it all around into a heart-led, personal values-based business that *feels good to run*?

Cultivating Self-Trust & Leaning into Discomfort

Before I dive into it all, know that the biggest thing is to cultivate a sense of trust in yourself, which will be covered in many ways throughout this book. It can take years of work. It will take journalling, coaching, inner work, healing, trying and failing to do it your way, taking brave action, making mistakes and relying on your future self to pick yourself up again when you do.

Something that supports me to lean into my way of running a business is to have regular big-picture business meetings with myself.[1] I reflect on how I feel, my values, and how I tie everything I do into my evolving philosophy. I also get clear on the practical side of things like my numbers, how I'm showing up, and the time I have available. I ask

---

[1] I share my full process for having "business meetings with myself" in my course, Clarify: https://ruthpoundwhite.com/clarify/

myself whether anything I'm doing feels "off" or "icky". I take time to tune into what's really going on under the surface.[2]

There's constant "noise" out there about new marketing tactics, or a push to always go bigger, to grow, to hire more people, to do more, more, more. It can feel hard to tune out that noise, but it gets easier the more you tune into yourself. If I see someone else doing something that I don't like, I take note of that, and I don't do it. If I'm being pulled in too many different directions, I remind myself to stay in my lane.

That's not to say we should never stretch our comfort zones, far from it. There's a difference between things that are *truly wrong for us* vs. those things that *feel wrong* **because we're scared**. So, when I talk about following what feels good (which will come up throughout this book), I don't mean that it necessarily always feels good – in the moment – to do so. This is where support and inner work comes in to help us distinguish where it's worth stretching in the name of who we really are and what we really desire to create, vs when it's worth holding back.

The truth is that it can also feel scary and uncomfortable to stay true to what you want. There's a reason why "blueprints" and listening to the online noise appeals to us on some level: it's because it's hard to trust your instincts, and it's scary to be the one responsible for making all the decisions. When you're just getting started, you don't know what you don't know yet. Even when you have some experience under your belt, there are so many unknowns when it comes to running a business.

---

[2] And it was, in fact, during one of these "meetings with myself" that I came up with the term "quietly ambitious"!)

If someone says you should try this latest marketing fad, what if you don't and everything goes wrong?

Defining Your Own Version of Success

I love social media, and I've made some beautiful connections through it, but it is difficult not to compare your worst bits with everyone's best bits. You see someone who looks like they've got it all figured out, and they're running their business in a certain way, and your brain latches onto that evidence of "what works". It's natural and human, but it becomes a problem when it constantly distracts you from your unique magic and your unique way of doing things. I'm not afraid to admit that I make great use of the mute and unfollow buttons for this reason. It's no reflection on them, it's about creating space to focus on my own ideas, and to define my own version of success.

When you define your own version of success – when you pause to ask yourself whether you *really* want that thing that everyone else is posting about, or whether you *really* want your work hours to look like theirs – everything gets easier.

Any time you find yourself chasing arbitrary goals, like a number of Instagram followers or certain levels of income, ask yourself why, or what for? What is it about having 10,000 Instagram followers that would make you feel good? If it's because you're publishing a book and the publisher needs to see evidence of your own audience, then fair enough. But if it's because so-and-so, who also does a thing similar to you has 10,000 followers and you don't feel good compared to them, then that's an arbitrary definition of success. It doesn't matter, and nobody is keeping score.

The truth is there aren't any specific rules. If you run your own online business, what you're doing is so new that you get to make things up as you go – and that's both the scariest and most liberating thing. Fourteen years ago, when I first started working online, I couldn't have imagined the direction it would take me in from then to now. Instagram wasn't even invented when I started! You have no idea what will change in this industry, or what you're capable of and what's possible for you. Let that be the reminder you need to design your business on your terms as you go.

Mistakes will happen along the way. But as online business owners we have the luxury of being able to test things quickly. For example, you can create a course, and if it doesn't work, or if the way you sell it doesn't work, you can try again in a different way. It's not the end of the world (in fact, it's a *good* thing that you learnt something about what *doesn't* work – we'll talk more about that in the chapter on failure).

Nobody else is running your business or living your life. Even if you have employees or you pay contractors, no one else knows your unique business like you do. **It is okay for you to run your business in the way that feels best and serves your life.** Cultivating trust, doing the inner work as outlined in this book, and getting clear on what matters to you is what will allow you to tune out the noise.

CHAPTER 2: ON BEING A HIGHLY SENSITIVE INTROVERT IN ONLINE BUSINESS

I've always been an introvert, but I didn't always know it.

I hate small talk. I get totally exhausted after certain social situations (despite enjoying many of those situations). I recharge my energy with time spent alone, rather than time spent with others. I'd often rather stay at home than go out with other people (and I am quite relieved when plans get cancelled).

These are all classic traits of an introvert[3], yet growing up I had absolutely no idea what an introvert was.

Side note: This chapter is about my experience as an introvert in business, but it's not *just* for other introverts to read. If you're an extrovert or an ambivert (somewhere in between introversion and extroversion) then there's still plenty to take away from running some aspects of your business like an introvert when that serves you, and playing to your own unique and equally brilliant strengths in other ways. I see you, and this book is as much for you as it is for the introverts.

---

[3] Some other common traits of introversion include: being reflective and self-aware, taking time to make decisions, favouring writing over speaking, disliking group work or being in a crowd, having few friendships, going "inwards" to rest.

Understanding Introversion & High Sensitivity

It's difficult to find exact numbers either way, but studies show that, while introversion is common, you are more likely to be born an extrovert who derives their energy from social interactions, making introverts a minority.[4]

There's also a known "extroversion bias" – a preference towards more typically extroverted personality traits[5] – thanks to the fact that extroverts are more likely to have larger numbers of friends, and are therefore likely better represented in our own friendship groups. Thanks to this bias, most of us know and understand that extroverts love spending time with other people, but may have had no idea about introversion growing up.

However common – or not – we may be, most introverts can relate to feeling "weird" or like an outsider for wanting to stay home rather than meet friends, or for feeling exhausted even after having a good time with other people. And, because we tend to be quieter, and certain cultures and settings are more geared to extroversion, we don't tend to hear so much about it.

---

[4] There is debate around how many people are *truly* introverted or extroverted. Research suggests that the largest group are those who sit somewhere in between: the ambiverts.

[5] Common traits of extroversion include: making quicker decisions, more likely to be seen as outgoing, and thriving in team or group settings.

When I uncovered my introversion at the age of 25, I had already been running my business for four years.

In her book *Quiet: The Power of Introverts in a World That Can't Stop Talking,* Susan Cain laid out the many ways that introverts have been misunderstood and undervalued. She describes the many ways in which our culture is largely designed for extroverts, including schools and workplaces, and argues that there is power in being shy, sensitive and quiet.

Reading *Quiet* was my first experience in getting to know and accept my introverted ways. I wasn't weird! I wasn't wrong (despite being told, over and over again, that I was "too quiet" at school)! This was a real "thing"! And, just maybe, I didn't need to fight against it in my life and business.

The experience opened the doors to a deeper interest in who I was, and I dug further with the Myers-Briggs Type Indicator (a popular personality test) via the website 16personalities.com. I am an INFJ – "The Advocate" – which is described on that website as follows[6]:

"[Advocates] tend to approach life with deep thoughtfulness and imagination. Their inner vision, personal values, and a quiet, principled version of humanism guide them in all things."

As an INFJ, I have a strong desire to make a positive difference in the world, to help people, to be of service, and to effect change. Although this is by no means unique to the INFJ personality type, reading these words in the results of that personality test really helped me to own this part of myself. I'm idealistic, and that's no bad thing.

---

[6] See https://www.16personalities.com/personality-types

Despite INFJ being the rarest personality type of all, we tend to congregate online, and that is one of the things I love most about the internet. I recommend you take the test for yourself: it's hugely validating to see yourself described in this way, and it's a powerful reminder that everyone has different strengths (we need them all).

Years later I discovered the concept of sensitivity and being a highly sensitive person (which is not limited to introverts). According to the research of Elaine Aron, high sensitivity means that "you are more aware than others of subtleties", "you are also more easily overwhelmed" and "it is innate" (biologists have found high sensitivity in over 100 species). Many highly sensitive people would also describe themselves as empaths (someone who is more sensitive to the emotions of others).

The website HSPerson.com gives us some screening questions[7]. For example:

- Do you get rattled when you have a lot to do in a short amount of time?
- Do you make a point of avoiding violent movies and TV shows?
- Do you need to withdraw during busy days into a darkened room or into bed?
- Do you make it a high priority to arrange your life to avoid upsetting or overwhelming situations?
- Do you have a rich and complex inner life?
- When you were a child, did your parents or teachers see you as sensitive or shy?

---

[7] See https://hsperson.com/test/

- Do you notice or enjoy delicate or fine sense, taste, sounds, or works of art?

If you answered yes to these questions, you might be highly sensitive.

Introverted, highly sensitive, empath... maybe you identify with these kinds of labels, maybe not. But bringing awareness to who you are and understanding your personality better is the first step in learning to work with it.

Working With Your Personality in Your Business

It's easy to focus on what we're lacking compared to the brilliant extroverts we see around us, but there are so many gifts of being highly sensitive or introverted too. You may get overwhelmed very easily, you may lose your energy in social situations, but you're also thoughtful, you're a good listener, and you think very deeply about things. When you do have something to say as an introvert, you're drawing on a whole host of strengths that give you so much to offer, which means that what you're saying is probably worth listening to.

We sensitive introverts also have the ability to connect with people on a deep level. We might find it hard to schmooze at a big event but, when we do connect with people, we have the ability to go deep, fast (which is probably why I enjoy podcasting so much – I can dive into those deep topics without all the "small talk" – an introvert's nightmare).

Being an introvert is also a superpower when it comes to doing work that means something. The more we own that, the more we give permission for others to do the same.

It's one thing having the awareness, though, and quite another to put it into action. It takes courage to choose to run your business your way, especially when the dominant voices are preaching something different.

In the early days of my business, I saw other people doing things a certain way and thought *that's the way it has to be done*. When I started in 2008, having an online business was way less "normal" than it is now and I didn't know anyone else "in real life" doing what I was. I learned from whoever I found online, not realising that some ways of working were not a good (or even healthy) fit for my personality.

I beat myself up about not wanting to go to networking events. I thought I was "less-than" for finding it hard to show up on video. I judged myself for keeping super private while visibility seemed to come naturally to others. I just didn't understand why simple things were so *hard* for me to do – and I thought it was because I wasn't good enough.

I have so much compassion for who I was back then. I was young, I barely knew myself, and I was building a totally new type of business that I'd never even heard of until I stumbled into it. I didn't factor being an introvert into the way I ran my business because I didn't factor anything about the way I felt into the way I ran my business.

Not only did I need to learn who I was, I also needed to *own* who I was, and I needed the courage to do things differently when how I felt wasn't compatible with some of the dominant business advice.

What it took to do that was a lot of learning and finding the right support. Early coaches didn't "get" me, I made a lot of mistakes and I followed a lot of advice that left me anxious, depleted, and feeling like a failure for not being able to do it the way other people did.

Having What It Takes & Stretching in the Name of What's Right

Underlying everything was the thought that I didn't have what it took to be a successful business owner.

I wasn't the right kind of person. I couldn't force myself to do what was required of me. There were certain things that you needed to be and do as a business owner, and those things weren't possible for me. Or so I thought.

Even calling myself a "business owner" took me many years. I was working with clients around the world, making good money and building my team, and I still couldn't fully acknowledge what I had created.

Eventually, and it's hard to admit this, it was reaching a certain level of income that finally validated the way I did things. Looking back, it seems absurd that I tied my self-worth as a business owner and the meaning of owning a business to earning a specific amount of money. But now, having worked with hundreds of business owners as a coach, I can see it's far more common than I thought.

Once I realised that I had to define for myself what it meant to be a "real business owner", I made the conscious decision to push my comfort zone in the name of what was right for me. I'm now very at peace with not doing certain things in my business (like networking!), and I'm also very willing to test the limits of what I think I'm capable of.

Before I owned my introverted nature it was unthinkable for me to be visible, to show my face and share my voice. I was trying to fit into a mould that just wasn't "me": in my first business I was never able to show up fully as myself, and I was never able to build an audience in the right way that made me feel comfortable enough to show up authentically. It was a vicious cycle.

Interestingly enough, after accepting who I was and deciding that I could do visibility in my own way, I was finally able to stretch my comfort zone massively. From interviewing other people on my podcast, to coaching and mentoring clients in groups and 1:1, and even showing my face on live video, I'm now showing up as my fully introverted self, and I've built an audience around that.

The best thing about showing up fully as myself is that anyone who works with me knows exactly who I am. If they don't like it, they don't work with me, and that works for me.

Visibility & Selling as an Introvert

Most introverts will agree that "showing up" consistently as a business owner can be hard as an introvert. Even when you're not specifically having conversations with lots of people, being visible for your business is still energetically demanding.

First, you need to trust that people actually need to hear what you have to say. It's normal to doubt yourself, especially as an introvert who is used to keeping yourself to yourself. *Will they like this? Will they find it annoying? Am I repeating myself too much? Is this even interesting?*

Showing up with trust is especially important during times when we need to sell or launch. As you'll learn in more detail in a later chapter, it's okay to want to hide away sometimes, and the more I've accepted being an introvert, and the more I've accepted and adapted my business to the necessary hiding away, the better it has been.

Fighting your need to hide away sometimes will only lead to hiding away more. Instead, be curious about what that need to hide is trying to tell you. Is there something you're resisting that you're afraid of? Or do you simply need to honour your energy right now? The best thing about owning who you are and being honest about it is that you can practice saying what you need. And if you need to introvert (yes, I'm using introvert as a verb), you need to introvert.

What can help is putting things into place before you launch or sell something. That can look like planning content in advance, writing down post ideas or scheduling emails. It can look like clearing your calendar so that you have more space to rest than usual. Whatever you do, do something to make it easier for yourself. Because when you don't plan ahead, you're way more likely to do yourself and the thing you're selling a disservice.

Every time I get burned out writing on social media and showing my face, I remind myself that the most amazing tool I have at my disposal as an introvert in my business is my email list. It's the introvert's dream. I love connecting with people through my email list, and getting vulnerable in my newsletters feels a lot safer in an enclosed community. Not to mention the fact that I can write in advance and have emails scheduled to go out while I'm far away from my computer (I even made money when I was in labour thanks to pre-scheduled emails!)

Email marketing is my number one tool when it comes to being an introvert in business, and that's what we'll be talking about in the next chapter. For now, I'll say that we can use email marketing to sell in a new way.

We need to change the way we think about selling. A lot of marketing is designed around our fears, making us feel less than good enough, even literally using psychological tactics that have been tested to manipulate people into making rash decisions. As sensitive humans, that's not the way we do things.

At its core, selling is about having something to offer. You share with people what it is, and allow them to make an empowered decision around whether that offer brings value into their life or whether it's not for them right now.

If you're a sensitive business owner, you're thoughtful, and you're coming from a place of service, offering something to the world that can help someone in some way. We get to remember that whenever selling starts to feel hard. And we get to redefine the way that we sell.

However you choose to show up, the key is to make your plan when the energy is there, and sell in your unique and soulful way without needing to show up every minute of every day.

Managing Your Energy

When you stretch your comfort zone bit by bit, things that used to terrify you quickly become easy. But, as an introvert, it doesn't change the fact that it takes energy to put yourself out there. It takes energy to talk to and be around people. And it requires recharging time.

Some of the ways I protect my energy as an introvert in my business include:

- Only allowing client calls or podcast interviews to happen on set days of the week, so that I have plenty of days fully free from calls

- Aiming to book calls close together in any given day, so that I don't have a big gap of time in between where I use up all my energy "thinking about it"
- Batching interviews for different seasons of the podcast so that I can focus my energy for a short period of time before recharging
- Allowing myself to have regular breaks from sharing on social media, especially when I experience a "vulnerability hangover"
- Never doing calls on a Monday (or else I'll think about them on the weekend)
- Working with a very small number of clients 1:1 but at a higher rate, to reflect how deep we go (and because I just can't handle a week full of 10 client calls!)

It's all about having boundaries and noticing where something is becoming too much.

Here is something I encourage all of my clients to do: Write down any times you feel anxious or uncomfortable in the day-to-day running of your business. Those negative feelings are often an indication that you need a new boundary. Once you set that boundary, it's a lot easier to stick to the level that feels good for you.

I also say no to a lot of things, as long as it's not purely out of fear. Business is uncomfortable, and stretching your comfort zone *is* scary. So ask yourself whether it would be right to turn down an opportunity from a place of knowing yourself and the energy it would take. If you find yourself saying no from a place of fear – even though the thing you're considering might make sense in the bigger picture of what you want to create in your business – then it might be time to gently stretch yourself.

Everything Is Possible for You

Before we finish off this chapter, it's important to note that all labels can have positive or negative associations. I am proud to be an introvert. I accept it and I own it. I don't think I'll ever *not* be an introvert, but I'm open to the possibility that things can change. I'm also open to the fact that more is possible for me than I ever thought.

In the past, I thought that being an introvert meant that certain things were categorically *not for me*. At the beginning of the chapter, I wrote about thinking that I *couldn't* do business because I didn't want to do it in a certain well-trod, loud way. Don't let your personality act as a barrier to what you might be capable of doing.

For example, I always wanted to create a podcast. But podcasting wasn't for "someone like me". Well, I did it. And the process made me realise that I had no idea what I was capable of as a shy introvert. It was possible to be socially awkward, to find it incredibly hard to talk to strangers at a networking event, AND still enjoy talking to selected guests on my podcast. In fact, I now couldn't imagine *not* podcasting.

You contain multitudes. Allow yourself to be surprised at what you can do and enjoy.

I've talked about shaping your business and your schedule around your introversion. I've touched on selling as an introvert. I've written about the benefits of being an introvert, caring a lot, and getting deep about what you do. The most important lesson that I would like you to come away with is that *sometimes you're going to forget that it's okay to be an introvert*.

Sometimes you're going to forget that it's okay to have the personality that you have in all its unique wonder. You're going to forget that it's fine that you're not like the "girl bosses". You're going to forget that it's fine that you're not who you always thought a business owner "should" be. You're going to forget that it's fine not to go to that conference that everyone else is going to, and you're going to forget that it's fine to do business your way.

Remind yourself that you are perfect, exactly as you are.

There are many ways to run a successful business. So much of what we're doing is all still so new, and most of us are just making it up as we go along (in the most wonderful way). There is no blueprint for this. You get to play by your own rules, and nobody else can tell you that what you're doing is wrong (even if the messages that you generally come across in society make you feel like that sometimes).

Wherever you fall on the personality spectrum, you have a unique set of strengths. Use them to your advantage. This is what I call your unique magic – the thing that makes you stand out from everybody else who does what you do. Only you can do that thing you do in the exact way you do it, so embrace that and offer yourself the support you need to make that possible. Get support from other people who understand. Put boundaries in place to protect your energy. Experiment. Mess things up until you find a way that works. And, whatever you do, keep talking about what it means to be an introvert, and give permission to others to show up in all their imperfect glory too.

CHAPTER 3: THE SOULFUL, SIMPLE, AND EFFECTIVE WAY TO DO EMAIL MARKETING

As a quietly ambitious entrepreneur, email marketing has always been my secret weapon.

I've been using email marketing in my businesses since 2008. For most of that time, it was the main way I made money, and I built a six-figure business almost entirely on email marketing. To me, there's nothing that compares with email marketing for highly sensitive business owners. Not convinced? Then keep reading.

Before I dive in and share what I've learned over a decade of email marketing, here's a basic definition (because the phrase itself – "email marketing" – might sound a bit cold and "sales-y"): *Email marketing describes the use of emails by business owners to promote or sell their products and services.*

If that definition doesn't resonate with you, try this: *Email marketing is a way for us to connect with our right people.*

Because that's really all it is at its core: it's about cultivating relationships with the people who resonate with the work you do, with the people who will *benefit* from the work you do.

The focus is often on the number of subscribers and, yes, growing your list size is great – but more importantly it's about the *quality* of those relationships. Building an *engaged* email list, full of people who are genuinely interested in what you do, is the aim of the game.

Why Email Marketing?

Almost all of my clients and business colleagues have a love-hate relationship with social media. Social media has helped me find my people, and I am eternally grateful for that. But it comes at a cost: the mindless scrolling, the comparison triggers, the bloody Instagram algorithm. The bottom line is that while social media can be great for business, it isn't always great for my mental wellbeing.

Email marketing is different. It's the heart of my business. Here's why I love it:

- It's something under your control, unlike a social media following built on another platform (where an algorithm shift or a random ban could instantly remove your reach without warning), you own your email list and can back it up and move it to another service provider at any time should you need to.
- It's something that people actively opt into. The fact that people give you their name, email, and permission to send them your content is magical. And the more they see your name in their inbox – even if they don't read every single email – the more you build an intimate relationship.
- The thing I love most about email? It's easy. You may not believe it (yet), but the way I use email makes my life and business easier. Email marketing is good for my work-life balance and good for my mental health. Yes, it may take time to get your head around the tech and to find your unique rhythm, but everything gets easier once you do.
- I love nothing more than scheduling a bunch of emails, shutting down my computer and forgetting about that thing that I'm

launching (versus showing up on social media, checking for comments, checking how many likes I've got compared to other people, seeing how other people are doing, going down a rabbit hole of comparison, and feeling crap about myself).

Don't just take my word for it about the power of email marketing. Here are some statistics to keep you motivated:

- In his book, *Company of One,* Paul Jarvis (who has an incredible email list of his own) makes the point that email marketing allows for infinitely "scaling without scale". It takes the same effort to email one person as it does 50,000 people.
- Email converts higher than other types of marketing: "If you had 1,000 followers, 1,000 organic visitors, and 1,000 email subscribers, and you tried to sell your offer to all of them, you could expect to convert 5.9 followers, 24.9 searchers, and 42.4 subscribers." – Meera Kothand, *300 Email Marketing Tips: Critical Advice And Strategy To Turn Subscribers Into Buyers & Grow A Six-Figure Business With Email*
- People have consistently stated that email is their preferred channel for promos over social media, and the average email open rate is 22% compared to an average social media engagement rate of 0.58%![8]
- According to Agency Analytics[9]: "more than half of internet users (58%) check their email first thing in the morning – before looking at Facebook, doing a Google search, or even

---

[8] See https://optinmonster.com/email-marketing-vs-social-media-performance-2016-2019-statistics/

[9] See https://agencyanalytics.com/blog/social-media-vs-email-marketing

checking the weather – and almost 9 out of 10 email users check their inbox at least once a day."

In short: email is the best way to put yourself in front of people, it's the preferred way to sell to them, and when you receive an email in your inbox (vs. pass by a social media post on your feed), you're far more likely to pay attention to it.

There is no "one way" to do email, just like there is no one way to do anything in your business. And as a sensitive human reading this book, I know that you might have a fear of email marketing being icky, too "salesy", or way too much work.

Email Marketing, Your Way

The one belief about marketing that I'd really love for you to come away with after reading this book is this: **it is possible to do any kind of marketing in your own way.**

There are many systems that make our business easier, but that are marketed or used and experienced in a way that doesn't resonate with us, so we avoid using them altogether.

What if, instead of avoiding these marketing techniques altogether, we asked whether there was a better way *for us*? It's not your fault that you've been on the receiving end of pushy marketing campaigns or spammy emails, but you get to decide now to do it differently.

Give yourself permission to use the tools that will make your life as a sensitive business owner easier. And give yourself permission to do it in your way.

As a sensitive business owner, the likelihood of you ever being "too salesy" is slim to none. And if you have fears about selling that get in the way of you actually selling what you do, email will make it all easier.

You can sell what you do like a human who cares about people *and* wants to get well paid.

Being yourself and doing things in alignment with your values is key to nurturing a true connection with your people.

Email marketing is an extension of how you show up in all other areas of your business. If you don't do it your way, if you're forcing yourself to follow a formula, blueprint, or pushy sales sequence that someone has told you always works and it doesn't feel right, then it's going to work against building a connection with your subscribers.

The Golden Rule teaches us to "do as you would be done by". It's a useful question to ask yourself, *would I like someone marketing to me in this way?* If not, don't do it. For example, maybe you don't mind when people send you emails about new products all the time, maybe you do, but neither of those options is right or wrong. Using the Golden Rule is a way to figure out what's right or wrong *for you*.

If you've been in the online business and marketing world for a while, you will hear all sorts of noise out there about how you've got to do "this", otherwise you're leaving money on the table, or you've got to do "that", otherwise your business won't work. While there are pushy and direct tactics that work to bring in more income sometimes, it's not anything that you can guarantee with any kind of formula. Don't think that you need to do things like XYZ marketer out there. Do things your way, and ultimately that will work for you.

I want to add a caveat here. Doing things your way doesn't mean you should hide away and not bother with email marketing. I'm hoping that after reading this chapter, you might be convinced that it's worth trying. When you do try it, you can take or leave my advice based on how you feel. I want to encourage you to try new things and push yourself out of your comfort zone in terms of marketing and selling what you do, but not to the extent that it doesn't feel in alignment with your values.

Selling Via Email (The Sensitive Way)

When I started my first business, I put off building my email list because of the cost. That was a mistake. Because once I started paying that monthly subscription fee, my email list became my biggest driver of sales and more than paid for itself (and is also the reason why I prioritised email from day 1 in my second business).

But how do you actually sell in email? How do you invite people to buy your offers while still building meaningful relationships with your subscribers?

My best advice for selling is to make what you have to offer a part of the wider conversation. This includes your social media posts, your blog posts, your podcast, your email newsletter, and anywhere else you show up.

Not every email you send is going to be a sales email. Equally, it's ok to sell in every email. I include links to my work in every email, technically meaning I "sell" in every email I send. But most of my emails are like blog posts, sharing a helpful lesson or insight with my subscribers – they're not *purely* selling something.

If you're uncomfortable about selling, start including links to work with you in every email (and blog post, podcast episode etc). Even if you change nothing else about your content, that alone will ensure that your right people know what it is that you do, and how they might work with you. It won't negatively affect your open rates, it won't tarnish the relationship you have with your people, but **it will make it easier for the right people to work with you.**

We often assume that everyone already knows about everything that we do. You've mentioned it on social media, you talked about it once in an email, surely that's enough? Time and time again I have launched something new, shared about it daily for a week, only to have people email me after the launch is over to say they missed it. Which is why it's important to direct people to your offers, and often.

Selling more often means you are probably, at some point, going to get the feeling that you've talked about your offer "too much". Just because you have that thought, that doesn't make it true. The fact is that you are the *only* person who pays this much attention to how many times you mention it. Nobody else will see every single thing you post on the internet.

Email makes it far easier to sell more often (and it quickly gets more comfortable the more you do it). When I schedule emails in advance, I can switch off from the fact that I'm selling come the time the emails actually go out. Let's say I'm launching something over the period of 7 days. I'll schedule out emails for most of those 7 days (if not every single day), but writing them in advance means I don't get sick of hearing myself talk when that week actually comes around.

Many sensitive entrepreneurs tell me that they find it harder to sell via email than social media. I'd like to argue that it's far *easier* to sell via email.

If I'd been showing up to speak on social media instead, it's very easy to feel like I'm repeating the same thing, or "imposing" on my people. Or, on the flip side, maybe I don't feel like showing up and talking on Stories one day – but if I've already got an email scheduled I can relax knowing that I am still putting my offer out there in front of my right people.

Although both email and social media can be scheduled in advance, this is far easier to automate with email. And scheduling in advance means that you get to have periods where you show up, and periods where you rest – essential for introverts, sensitive humans, and anyone with physical or mental limitations on their time and energy.

Don't forget that social media algorithms can change at any time. Different platforms go in and out of fashion with different people (anyone remember MySpace?). And profiles can be blocked or banned with no notice. This doesn't mean you shouldn't be showing up on social media too, if you enjoy it, it simply means that the smart option is to direct as many people from your social platforms towards your email list. In other words: don't put all of your eggs in somebody else's basket.

Writing Emails & Inviting People to Subscribe

Another common objection I hear from clients is that email marketing adds a whole other massive thing to their to do list: the need to come up with new content every week.

Firstly, if you feel this pressure, I would suggest writing less frequently if that makes things easier for you. I write my newsletter weekly, but there are plenty of people who send newsletters monthly or every two weeks. And remember that you can always start monthly and change to write more often once you find your groove. It's better to send emails less frequently than to not send them at all. If you send an email monthly people will still remember who you are.

Secondly, give yourself permission to experiment and find your voice, find your flow, find your rhythm, and see what works best for you. I can't give you a golden formula of how often you should write, how long those emails should be and what they should include. For sensitive business owners, the only way this gets to be sustainable is the way that works best *for you* as a human.

Thirdly, it's okay to repurpose your content. Not everything you send to your email subscribers has to be brand new and unique. If you're reading this book then I'm guessing you're not a huge firm with a massive marketing budget and hundreds of employees. There is only so much that we have the energy and the time to do, so make the most of the content you write and share it on different platforms, and re-share it at different times. The fact is that most people who follow us are not going to see absolutely everything we ever post or every single email we send (which, by the way, is reason enough to repurpose: to make sure that more people see it). Those that do see it more than once are not going to care – I promise.

If you regularly write blog posts, or long text-based social media posts, then you can re-use them too. Granted, some subscribers may already read your posts on social media and prefer to unsubscribe if they're not getting original content, but some others may never have seen your content had you not shared it in both places.

Here's how it might work with my own newsletters: I'll often write a newsletter and post a part of it on Instagram. Sometimes I'll invite followers there to sign up to my newsletter to read it in full. It saves me time, but it's also a way of saying: *did you know I had a newsletter? Come and join me there too!* Occasionally I will take an email newsletter I've written and publish it as a blog post and invite people through the blog post to sign up to my newsletter. And if I don't repurpose or repost any of the content *now*, I'll still save it in a Google doc to repurpose at a later date.

Do you see how it's all connected?

This way of sharing content also ties back into making your email list a part of the wider conversation of your whole business, and the heart of the ecosystem of content that you're putting out there. I encourage all of my clients and followers to mention their email newsletter often.

Another suggestion is to "tease" a newsletter as you're writing it, before it goes out. Share on Instagram Stories and invite people to sign up before it goes out on a specific day. Sometimes I'll tell people exactly what it's about, sometimes it'll be more of a tease (for example, *I'll be sharing a juicy behind-the-scenes update on how my last launch went – subscribe if you want all the numbers*).

Ultimately the way you write to your email list is going to come down to how you feel about it and how much time you've got. I encourage you to tune out the noise and to allow yourself to figure things out as you go.

And remember, there are no rules. Do you need a complex landing page to gain subscribers? No, you need a simple sign-up form to get started. Do you need a valuable freebie to entice people to join? No, you can simply tell them what you're going to write in your newsletters (in a way that speaks to how that benefits your reader). Do you need many thousands of people subscribed to build a successful business and make good money? No, and my business is proof of that.

It doesn't mean you won't want any of those things at some point. But I hope that it encourages you to start writing and inviting people to read your newsletters imperfectly without waiting until everything's perfect first. Doing *anything* imperfectly is so much better than not doing anything at all.

Speaking of which, let's talk about getting started in the simplest way possible.

Getting Started Without The Stress

I have helped over 1000 people kickstart their email marketing without stress and drama, and I invite you to sign up to my email resources if you want a little accountability to get going (your way, of course):

- Download my free checklist "**the 6 stages of growing your email list** (the simple & soulful way!)" at ruthpoundwhite.com/emailchecklist
- Opt into the **free 5-day "soulful & simple list building" challenge** (for a little more accountability to get the work done) at ruthpoundwhite.com/emailchallenge
- Or sign up to my full **soulful email marketing course**, Cultivate http://ruthpoundwhite.com/cultivate-course/

My best advice for getting started is to first decide that it's worth setting aside a little time to focus on the tech that'll get you up and running. A lot of the tech is a one-time hurdle, and it gets so much easier very quickly.

Next, sign up with an email marketing service provider (you could spend hours researching the different options, but I recommend

ConvertKit[10]). Once you've signed up, either create a landing page or add a subscription form to your website (if website code freaks you out, creating a landing page using your email provider template is the path of least resistance at first). This is where you'll direct people to sign up to your newsletter.

Don't just call it a "newsletter". Think of a reason why people would subscribe to your email updates. Consider the benefit of reading your emails and speak to that when you invite people to subscribe. For example, it could be a look behind-the-scenes of whatever you're working on. It could be first access to sales if you sell products. It could be your personal thoughts and behind-the-scenes access that you don't share outside of your newsletter... anything.

Once you've set up your landing page, or subscription form on your website, link to that page from all of your social media profiles and start inviting people to your newsletter.

And that is the simplest way to get started with email marketing. Doesn't sound too bad, does it?

The key thing is that you take that step, sign up and find a way for people to subscribe to your newsletter. You can worry about all the other details later. It is so worth doing this work – it will make your business life so much easier. I love the act of writing my newsletters, and I love the results that they give me.

---

[10] This is an affiliate link - https://ruthpoundwhite.com/l/convertkit - meaning that if you do sign up, I'll receive a small commission if you go on to become a paid member. I've been using ConvertKit since 2015 and highly recommend them.

Sensitive Email Marketing Q&A

As a business mentor, I get a lot of questions about email marketing. I've decided to put this section in Q&A format with some of my audience's most frequently asked questions.

Q. Is it worth writing regularly if you have a tiny list?

A: One of the hardest things about email marketing – and, in fact, any kind of marketing – is putting all the work in when you only have a tiny audience. The fact is that everyone starts at zero.

"Numbers" are tricky aren't they? It's hard not to care about them, even though we know it's really more about quality than quantity. Thankfully it's far easier not to care about the numbers with email marketing. Unlike social media followers, nobody else knows how many subscribers you have. As far as your subscribers are concerned, you are writing only to them – and this is a very helpful mindset to keep in mind when you are putting all your efforts into writing for a tiny list.

Don't delay writing to your email list because it's "too small". I remember committing to writing weekly newsletters when I had just four subscribers. I started making money from my emails with well under 100 subscribers. And I was able to make a healthy six-figure income from a list of around 3000. I have never had a huge list, and that is the power of heart-led marketing. You don't need to reach masses and masses of people! You simply need to connect with the *right* people.

Having the right people subscribed and writing the right kind of content that fosters a deep connection means that you do not have to have a big email list at all for it to be impactful in terms of connecting with people, and to make your whole business life easier and more sustainable.

Q: How often should you show up in people's inboxes?

A: It probably won't surprise you to learn that I don't have a definitive answer for this one. It comes down to a few things. Firstly, you've got to be realistic with yourself and think about what you can commit to. It's all very well and good to want to show up in people's inboxes twice a week, but if you're going to find that stressful – and if that stress is going to lead to you petering out and not doing it at all – then that's probably not a good idea.

If you're new to sending an email newsletter, then it's also important to accept that there will be a learning curve. For example, with my email newsletter, I started with very good intentions writing once a week, but I didn't know what I was doing and what exactly I wanted out of it, so I found it difficult to stay consistent. Sometimes I'd go weeks or months without writing. Then, once I got into the groove more, I decided that once a week probably was too much for me, so I shifted to once every two weeks, which became my sweet spot for a while.

When I was able to stick to the schedule more, it gave me the momentum I needed. Momentum meant that email newsletter became a regular part of all my work. Now I've gone back to weekly, and it's fine in terms of my workload and what I'm used to, because I know exactly what I'm doing with my email newsletter. It's easy for me to have something to say to people, but I'm not afraid to miss one if I need to, and I do that sometimes. I'm also not afraid to send extra emails sometimes if I have something special going on!

European data protection laws (GDPR) mean that it's important to be clear about what people are signing up to when they sign up to your newsletter. Obviously, I'm not a lawyer, so don't take this as legal advice, but I recommend you don't box yourself in by being too specific in how often you'll say you'll email. Let them know they're signing up to your email newsletters and, from time-to-time, promotional emails and freebies, and that covers you for everything.

Most importantly, your email schedule has to feel good for *you*. You can also bring the Golden Rule into play here. How do you react to other people's emails? Personally, I'm likely to unsubscribe from businesses that email me daily – it's just too much for my inbox. But as long as I'm genuinely interested in what someone has to say, I'm happy to receive emails from them anywhere from several times a week to once a month or every couple of months (any longer in between emails, though, and I might not remember who they are or why I subscribed in the first place).

When you do start emailing, remember that it's okay to change your schedule whenever you want to, as needed. Commit to something that feels right to you now, commit to doing it on at least a semi-regular basis, and over time you'll (a) make some changes to find a rhythm that really works for you and (b) totally see just how worth it that commitment has been.

Q: What does it mean when people unsubscribe?

A: As painful as it may feel at first, unsubscribes mean nothing about the value of your emails or the success of your business. It could mean that the person wasn't quite right for you and they are making space for more of the right people (which is good because you want to have an engaged email list, and you don't want to be paying for people who don't want to see what you have to say). And sometimes, it simply means somebody is having a clear out. They might still follow you elsewhere, they might come back at a later date. People are busy and have every right to unsubscribe and quieten things down whenever they feel like it.

You'll probably never know exactly why every person unsubscribes, and I encourage you not to create negative meaning when there might not be one. Unsubscribes aren't personal - they are a normal and natural part of marketing your business using email, and they don't mean that people don't like what you do.

Q: How do I generate content ideas and plan for content?

A: Firstly, don't put any pressure on yourself to see email content as anything different than content you put out there elsewhere. If you have a good system for coming up with content ideas on other platforms, that will translate to emails.

I have many ways to generate content ideas. I choose to write my newsletters a little differently than blog posts – it feels that little bit more personal. If you were to compare it to public speaking, it would be the difference between talking to the audience of my podcast and talking to an intimate room of people. This isn't a rule for all email newsletters, it's simply the way I choose to do it.

Because it feels more personal, I tend to write whatever I feel like at the time: things that I'm working on, behind-the-scenes updates, things I've found useful or inspiring, and how I'm feeling. Sometimes I'll still share the odd how-to or blog-like piece of content.

I keep track of my content ideas using a list on my phone – the same way I keep track of ideas for my podcast, blog or Instagram posts. I like using my phone because it's there whenever an idea strikes me.

I create content quite intuitively, meaning that it's important for me to feel "in the moment" when I write. That doesn't mean I don't write in advance: on the contrary, I find sitting down to a blank page and forcing myself to write a newsletter quite stressful. So keeping this running list of topic ideas and drafts feels like the best of both worlds for me, and I rarely run out of ideas.

If you are someone who likes to plan in advance and needs some more inspiration you could try looking at the most popular posts on your blog or Instagram and seeing what people resonated with, and noticing the questions that they're asking you. You might even be inspired by other people's email newsletters, books, magazine articles etc.

If you want to dive more into planning your content, I have an affordable e-book on the subject called *Spark*.[11] In it, I share the different techniques I use for generating content ideas in all areas, which you can use to generate a year's worth of content ideas.

Q: What email marketing service provider should I use?

A: There are many great service providers, but ConvertKit is the one I use and recommend[12]. They have a number of powerful features, including customisable automations and integrations with other services (like my shopping cart). ConvertKit allows you tag people with different subjects or remove people from different newsletters so that you can tailor the experience more.

---

[11] Available at ruthpoundwhite.com/spark-ebook

[12] This is an affiliate link - https://ruthpoundwhite.com/l/convertkit - meaning that if you do sign up, I'll receive a small commission if you go on to become a paid member. I've been using them since 2015 and highly recommend them.

Q. How do you create an email marketing strategy based on what your client needs? Should you do a survey or write from the heart and send whatever you want?

A. It depends on your area of business. If you're a creator and individual business owner, you have to find the balance between what you want and what your clients want. I'm all about building a business in a way that feels good and works around how you are as a person, and attracting your "right people" to you based on that.

Writing from the heart matters if you want a connection-based business. If you don't – and if you prioritise your subscribers' preferences ahead of your own - you'll put yourself into a box that isn't quite right for you. That's not to say that you can't survey your audience for ideas, or get inspired by the questions that they ask you. There's a balance to be struck between what you want and what your clients want.

Follow your heart and pay attention to how it's going, both in terms of how you feel and how much it resonates. It is useful to make a note when you get certain replies and when people start sharing your newsletter. What gets people opening newsletters and responding? What links are people clicking on?

Don't worry about getting it all completely right from the start. This is something that you're going to learn as you go. You're going to get a feel for it, and you're going to notice what resonates with people and what doesn't. Also, remember even if people don't reply to emails, it doesn't mean that it's not resonating with them (it's far less common for people to reply to emails than it is for them to leave a comment on social media).

Hopefully, this chapter has given you what you need to spend less time on social media and more time in people's inboxes. And, of course, more time introverting, if that's what you need.

And finally, don't forget my free email marketing resources if you need more guidance on getting going:

- Download my free checklist "**the 6 stages of growing your email list** (the simple & soulful way!)" at ruthpoundwhite.com/emailchecklist
- Opt into the **free 5-day "soulful & simple list building" challenge** (for a little more accountability to get the work done) at ruthpoundwhite.com/emailchallenge
- Or sign up to my full **soulful email marketing course**, Cultivate http://ruthpoundwhite.com/cultivate-course/

CHAPTER 4: 5 THINGS I WOULD TELL THE SUMMER 2018 VERSION OF ME

On June 16th, 2018, I created an Instagram account after 10 years of hiding in my business. Something in me told me it was time to get visible, it was time to start putting myself out there, it was time to start speaking my truth and being myself in my business.

I had no idea where it would lead me and what it would teach me.

At that time, I had a six-month-old baby. I had a hard time adjusting to motherhood, and I was also massively fired up to change the work that I was doing to make my son (and myself) proud.

By then I'd built up my copywriting business and watched it grow into a successful company that provided enough revenue to support my family, and my five-month maternity leave. By June of 2018, I was back to working in the business, but I knew it was time to put some big changes in motion.

"And the day came when the risk to remain tight in a bud was more painful than the risk it took to blossom."

– Anaïs Nin[13]

---

[13] Although widely attributed to Anaïs Nin, this line may have been authored by Elizabeth Appell. See:

That day came for me in the summer of 2018 when I started my Instagram account and began putting myself out there authentically. If I could go back to that time and tell that Ruth a few things, here's what I would say.

(1) "I am so bloody proud of you"

In June 2018 I'd come out of possibly the most challenging time of my life, adjusting to new motherhood. In hindsight, if all I had done was survived that time, that would have been enough. If you are a new parent and going through that experience right now, please hear me: surviving is enough.

I'm proud of myself for surviving, but I'm also proud of myself for being brave and deciding to put my face out there, to start sharing my voice and show up in the name of what was in my heart, even though I didn't know where it would lead (which is what this book is all about).

(2) "It's okay if you don't know what you're doing"

When I started my Instagram account in 2018, I didn't have anything to sell, and I didn't have anything planned to sell. Because of my own business journey, I vaguely knew at that point that I wanted to support people in their businesses – especially as sensitive and introverted humans. New motherhood had also taught me how

---

http://anaisninblog.skybluepress.com/2013/03/who-wrote-risk-is-the-mystery-solved

important it was for me to do work that fulfilled me and that meant something, *and I let myself figure out what that was as I went* (it wasn't until around 6 months later that I launched my first course and started working with clients 1:1 as a business coach & mentor).

I was fortunate that I had space to experiment at the time thanks to ongoing income from my copywriting business. By allowing myself to show up before I knew what I was showing up for I made connections, I built relationships, I grew my Instagram following, and I started my email newsletter.

That's not to say that it felt comfortable to start before knowing what I was doing, though. On the contrary, I remember feeling "stupid" sometimes, especially when followers would send me a message saying, *"I like what you're putting out there, but I don't understand what you do."* I would reply saying, *"I don't know what I do either."* That felt uncomfortable, especially since I knew I wanted to support others with their businesses. *Shouldn't I have it all figured out myself?*

Even when I did have an offer to sell, even when I figured out more specifically what I wanted to do, I remember desperately wanting to feel more clarity. This is something I have now seen again and again in the work I do with my own clients: wanting to know *exactly* who we're working with, what all our offers should be and what the purpose of it all is.

It's human nature to wish you could see the full picture from day one, but in hindsight I can see **it was part of my journey to figure it out as I went**, and it's totally normal for it to work this way. *Clarity comes through taking action, doing things imperfectly, and being willing to experiment.*

Looking back, it's been an incredible journey. Everything I went through, everything I did, and everything I tried have played into what

I'm doing now. I wouldn't change it. ***I would only go back and tell myself to have patience.***

(3) "You have no idea what you're capable of"

When I started putting myself out there in this new way, I was aware that I was being brave, and I gave myself credit for that, but I also saw limits to that bravery. I could show up on Instagram, for example, but I could never do a live video. Or I could share my words in an email newsletter, but not my voice in a podcast.

I'd had the nudge to do a podcast for a long time – since before I even started that Instagram account – and I had decided it wasn't for "someone like me". I knew I was being brave by sharing my thoughts on Instagram, I didn't think I could be *that* brave and, even if I was, it wouldn't be any good. (Can you relate to this way of thinking?)

I had similar thoughts about coaching and mentoring: *that's not for me, and I'm not even willing to try it* (in fact, it took all my courage just to write to my first coach, the brilliant Jen Carrington, to enquire about working with her).

The voice telling me those things weren't for "someone like me" was trying to keep me safe, but it was not speaking the truth. Thankfully, the "nudge" to try something new wouldn't go away, and I allowed myself to at least *imagine* trying it.

The "nudge" I felt is hard to describe, but I know that if you're reading this, you'll resonate when there's that something for you. When your brain is telling you it's not safe, or that you're not good enough, but there's a tiny part of you breaking through the noise that's still telling you *"I want to try that"*. Thank goodness for that part of me, because I really had no idea what I was capable of.

Starting my podcast was challenging. It brought up anxiety, it forced me to face my fears about how good (or not) I was at speaking to people, and I felt vulnerable putting my voice out there. It was uncomfortable following the nudge.

Despite the discomfort, when I released it, it felt so right.[14]

It blew my mind to have people say to me that I was *good* at podcasting, or that I had a nice voice. It went against everything my brain was used to thinking. I didn't know how capable I was.

As entrepreneurs, this is a lesson I think a lot of us have to learn again, and again, and again. I didn't know what I was capable of when I applied for my first freelance gig in 2008, I didn't know what I was capable of when I went travelling for a year in 2012, I didn't know what I was capable of when I became a mother in 2017, I didn't know what I was capable of when I put that first podcast episode out there, or started working with my first coaching client. And I still have no idea how capable I am.

Because of how scared I often felt in different situations, I never considered myself to be a brave person. But being brave isn't about never being scared; being brave is about doing things in spite of the fear. It's a lesson I have to learn again and again: *I'm capable.*

---

[14] If you want to hear more about my podcasting journey specifically, I shared it all in episode #22 of the Quietly Ambitious Podcast: https://ruthpoundwhite.com/episode-22-on-starting-something-new-scary-my-creatively-human-podcasting-journey/

Those experiences when I've been brave and surprised myself have shifted something in my brain. I have no idea what I'm capable of, which makes anything possible for me. That's pretty exciting.

(4) "Your right people are out there"

When I started my new Instagram account, I had just signed up to a course on visibility with Ray Dodd, and an Instagram course with Sara Tasker. It was the perfect time for me to get visible with my new Instagram account, but more than that I wanted to actually show up in those course communities.

I've always felt like a bit of an outsider, reluctant to open up to people, and a serial lurker in online spaces. These two courses really changed that for me. Both Ray and Sara have wonderful communities of like-minded humans surrounding them. I am still friends with people who I met in those two communities to this day, and I have met several of them in person, which is so, so special to me.

What I learned is that it wasn't until I was willing to be seen in these communities that I realised my people were there all along.[15]

We naturally get along differently with different people, but I've learned that we all have the same fears about putting ourselves out there, about running a business, or having a child or being a woman and wanting to earn a lot of money, and so on. But we never know

---

[15] This is something I spoke to Vicky Shilling about in episode #61 of the Quietly Ambitious podcast: https://ruthpoundwhite.com/episode-61-overcoming-fear-of-judgement-from-other-people-with-vicky-shilling/

unless we're willing to share. These communities – alongside connecting with my people on Instagram – taught me how to do that.

I'm glad that those communities exist online, and I'm sad that I didn't feel able to be seen in the past. If you're a lurker and you're reading this, then I encourage you to say hello. I want to know that I see you (even though I don't necessarily *see* you because you're lurking!), but I see you and I know what it's like. There is a lot to gain from taking that risk to show up and be seen in a community. So come and say hi on Instagram @ruthpoundwhite, or join the Facebook group[16], and don't be afraid to let me know that you're feeling shy – we don't judge here.

The same goes for showing up in your online content. Be honest that you've got feelings about showing up. People get it, it's human, and more people will resonate with that than you think. There's so much power in being open and telling the truth.

(5) "Finding your voice is a journey and not a destination"

Finding my voice has been a fulfilling journey that I wouldn't change, even if I could. The more I put my words out there, the more I develop my voice. It has been messy, it has brought up all of the feelings of fear and discomfort, it has made me want to hide away (many times), and it has led to many a "vulnerability hangover".

Some may argue that the "vulnerability hangover" is a sign that you're not saying what you really want to say, but I disagree.

---

[16] Get your invitation to the group when you sign up to the book bonuses at ruthpoundwhite.com/bookbonus

Sometimes it is a sign that I overstepped my own boundaries and shared too much (which I get to learn from.) Often, it's a sign that I am finding my voice, and I'm stretching what I feel safe to say in public. And it's all part of the journey.

Part of learning to show up authentically and wholeheartedly is about getting out there, trying things, letting it be an experiment, and seeing how it feels. The other part is about *deep* self-care, reflection and putting yourself first. The journalling, the therapy, the coaching, being willing to learn, being willing to think differently, and surrounding yourself with people who encourage you to stretch in the best way possible.

At this point, I know the journey is never done. A few years ago I was always looking to the next course, the next coach, the next strategy to be the one that would help me figure it all out. Now, I'm far more interested in what feels good to me right now, as well as what doesn't – and asking myself what boundaries or what beliefs I need to change as a result. As long as what I'm doing is feeling fulfilling and it's stretching me, I'm happy. It's the journey of continuous growth as a human.

In 2018, when I got visible and started my Instagram account, I honestly didn't think I had a voice. It makes me sad to look back, but it also makes me laugh. Because the truth is I have *so much* to say. I just didn't know how, I didn't feel safe, and I had suppressed it for too long.

Here I am now, helping other people to find their voice and step up and share what's in their heart, unapologetically, and all in a way that supports their well-being and expands the limits of what they believe is safe. So much of the work I do with my clients now is to help them learn to listen to themselves and to be okay with what they want (even if it feels uncomfortable).

> Want what you want.
>
> Know you deserve it.
>
> Know you're good enough for it.
>
> Keep doing what you're doing because your work really does matter.

CHAPTER 5: ON MAKING MISTAKES & LEARNING THE RIGHT LESSONS

Fear of failure is something that almost all of us have in common as sensitive business owners. It's easy to look at what others have done and think that everything just seemed to work out for them. The truth is, failure is a huge and unavoidable part of building a business.

I have made many mistakes and failed many times in my 14-year entrepreneurial journey. It took many years, but I'm finally ready and willing to fail *as a way to learn*. More and more, I'm also willing to fail in public – to be seen to make mistakes, because we all make them. I hope reading about my mistakes, and the lessons they led to, will allow you to be gentle with yourself when you inevitably fail too.

Here are some of my biggest failures in my online business journey (of course, I could also call them lessons learned):

(1) Failure to charge what I needed to charge

I did many kinds of work in the early years of my business. Copywriting was my bread and butter, but I tried many other things alongside this while I found my "thing". One of them was website development – not web design, but setting websites up for people, customising their WordPress theme and filling the site with content.

I was working on a website for a client after having just had to move, when our rental flat had been sold. It was a stressful and exhausting experience, but I felt that I couldn't take any time off work for the move.

I was working on this client's website, I didn't back it up, and... I accidently deleted the entire website from the file manager. There's no getting around the failure of erasing someone's site (luckily, *they* had a backup – which I should have had myself), and creating a load of extra work for myself. But that's not the failure I really want to share with you (we all make mistakes, after all, even if this one was especially bad).

The bigger failure was in charging what I really needed to charge. I was charging embarrassingly little, sometimes earning $20 to write an entire article written full of keywords for SEO. And, because of that, I had to take on a lot of work. I found it easy to get work, so it felt sustainable to rely on volume over raising my prices.

What I didn't realise at the time was that the reason I found it easy to get so much work was *because* I was cheap, and that I was better than other people who were that cheap. But I couldn't claim the value of what I did, *at all*. I had too many clients, I had referrals coming from all directions, I was overworking and I was aiming for bare minimum living expenses. But I still didn't feel able or worthy enough to raise my rates.

(I also had a huge belief that I had to work hard to earn my money. So hard, in fact, that I overworked myself to the point at which I was so tired I did mindless things like not backing up a client website and deleting the whole thing.)

It's so easy to fall into this trap, and I'm not shaming anybody for what they charge. In fact, there's nothing wrong with charging less than the market average when you're first starting out. It's valuable to get those first few clients and testimonials, and it can boost your confidence in the early days. The problem comes when you find yourself reaching burnout, and you can't believe that you're worth anything more.

The truth is that you can *never* charge your worth. Your value as a human cannot be measured. The real work with pricing comes in believing in the value that your work brings to your clients. And the truth is that aiming to be the cheapest means that the lowest price is the only thing your clients will value. When you start valuing what you offer beyond the cheapest price, you start to attract clients who value that too.

In the early days of my business my life was flexible, I didn't have a mortgage, I didn't have a child, and I told myself it was sustainable to work harder and longer to make more money. Looking back, it was a story about how much I deserved to receive based on my output. The shift would come from raising my prices and working on my mindset around "value" and "worth".

(2) Seeing everybody else as competition

When I first started my business I was jealous of other people and saw everyone as my competition. If my prices weren't evidence enough of my scarcity mindset and inability to see my own value in business, my attitude towards others definitely was. I didn't think that there was more than enough work out there for everyone, and I was always afraid that clients would choose my competition over me.

(On the flip side, I put some people on a pedestal and wanted to be *exactly* like. My extreme feelings towards others were a sign that there was a deeper self-worth issue going on that I needed to figure out about myself.)

Once I started to embrace community over competition, my business and my confidence grew. We referred clients to each other, we learned from each other, and we shared the same struggles and frustrations.

The biggest benefit was that we knew we didn't have to do it all alone. It is so important to have people around you who "get it" when you're working for yourself. We would come to each other with ideas for doing things differently, for moral support when we had difficult clients, or to cheer each other along and celebrate when things were going well.

(We also happened to make a lot of money by referring work in the direction of each other! Far more, I believe, than we would have done alone. And, when it came time to let go of my first business, it made it easy to find a buyer for my digital assets.)

(3) Not trusting my abilities as a business owner

I didn't trust my ability to charge more in my business, I didn't trust that I would stand out from my "competition", and I always felt I had to prove myself with how hard I worked. I'd love to tell you that I did the inner work and healing and learned, back then, that my self-worth was completely independent of my results, but I'd be lying.

It wasn't until the money started coming in larger amounts that I started fully owning just what I had created as a business owner. I don't blame myself for failing to see this independently – after all, I was young, I was shy, I was nervous and I was doing something brand new. But it was shocking and sad to realise just how little credit I had offered myself until the money came in.

When I started my coaching and mentoring business in 2018 I hadn't started working with any one-to-one clients yet and was figuring out what I really wanted to do. After building a six-figure business based primarily on email marketing for the last ten years, I decided that teaching email marketing was the best place to start. I put together a free email marketing challenge, and a couple of hundred people signed up for it (which I was thrilled with).

This was a brand new business with a very small audience, so the uptake for the free challenge made me hopeful that I'd sell many spaces in my full in-depth email marketing course. I put it out into the world and... crickets. I had a couple of messages from people who were interested but said it wasn't the right time. And so, instead of continuing to talk about it until the very end of the launch period (something I'm always telling my clients to do!), I just stopped talking about it. Because if people weren't buying it right away, they clearly weren't interested (or so I thought back then).

Despite the fact that I had a tiny audience (and it's normal to have 1-2% of people in your audience sign up to a paid offer), and despite the fact that I had stopped telling people about the offer altogether, I decided that I was a failure. I wasn't helping other people build their businesses, I wasn't even selling in my own business. I was a fraud.

Looking back, I can see that of course this wasn't true. No single launch can ever make you a failure in your business, and it's normal to have some (sometimes many) launches completely flop, especially early on. But I was also discounting my decade of experience in building a successful and profitable business based on email marketing.

Just because I didn't sell out a course with a very small audience the first time around does not make *me* – or my business – a failure. I eventually went on to relaunch this course several times, and have had 70 students go through live rounds at the time of writing, with others joining through an evergreen funnel that now requires no extra work on my part. And when I look back, it feels like the best thing that it didn't sell. Because what I ultimately created was much better than what I was originally planning. Not to mention the fact that I learned a valuable lesson from the launch failing.

(4) Taking years to do what was in my heart

In the previous chapter, I wrote about the decision I made to get visible in June 2018, ten years after first starting my freelance writing business. What I didn't make clear was that I had the desire to do this for at least three or four years before it actually happened.

It was clear to me a few years into my copywriting career that it wasn't my "forever" business. I'd set it up almost by accident, it had not been designed intentionally around who I was or what I valued. It made me good money, but that wasn't enough for this sensitive INFJ.

So I started taking courses and I made plans for a new business. I had ideas for trainings and courses and blog posts and podcasts. And I'd put something out there and hide away for months. Over and over again. It was one step forward, one step back, always returning to where I had been and what I was used to in my business.

Momentum is everything as a business owner. The early days of a new business are always some of the hardest, and it can feel as if you're getting nowhere until, suddenly, it starts to snowball. That is the power of building momentum with your visibility.

I didn't build any momentum with my new business idea until I went through a life-changing event in 2017. My world had been turned upside down and I found it so hard to adjust to new motherhood. It cracked me open and suddenly I found myself willing to throw everything at it.

From the outside it might look like that momentum built very quickly for me once I decided to get visible, and in some ways that's true. But it took years of failure to commit, failure to really go all in, failure to believe in myself to even get me to the point at which I was ready to decide *this is happening, no matter what.*

The Truth About Failure

None of these four examples of failure are *truly* failures. They all led to important realisations and important changes in my business. And when you've been in business for 14 years, it does get easier to fail because it's easy to look back at all your history and to know that whatever things you did in the past all led you to *exactly* where you are now (and if you want some proof and inspiration, just type "failures to success stories" into Google).

Even if I hadn't ultimately created a successful version of that course that didn't sell, that failure would have still taught me so much, still have supported me in connecting with my clients who will inevitably have some launches fail too and still have given me something to share with you now.

There is power in sharing our failures in public, even if it's hard. Doesn't it make it easier to know that we all fail, and we all *will* fail at some point? Doesn't it make it easier to know that we all have the same feelings and fears around failing? It also makes it easier to be more public about your goals, knowing that it's incredibly normal to fail on the way to reaching them.

The other thing about setting public goals is that some people will never think what you achieve is enough. This is where cultivating our own definition of success helps to build out sense of internal motivation. A few years ago, I ran the London marathon. That was a massive, massive achievement for me (I've never been a sporty person). I did it in under five hours, and it was interesting to hear the reaction any time somebody asked me how long it took me. I was proud of my achievement, regardless of any external judgement.

With internal motivation comes the risk of failing yourself. I believe that this, above all, is what often stops us from setting big goals and aiming for what we really want. What if we disappoint ourselves? What if we don't set out to do what we thought we could? What would that mean about us?

I used to be someone who struggled to set goals out of fear that I wouldn't meet them, even when there weren't any external repercussions. In fact, I found it hard to even admit what my biggest goals were, worried that they might have been wrong or not turned out as a I imaged.

It is an act of deep self-trust to allow yourself to truly want what you want, and to aim to make things happen despite the risk that it won't. In a past email newsletter, I wrote, "don't be afraid to set big goals because dreaming is free." If you're somebody who finds it hard to even "go there" with your goals, then I recommend setting yourself a recurring reminder using those words.

The failures, the mistakes and the dreams that don't quite happen are all part of the journey of being an entrepreneur and building up your business. Let's not run away from our fears and our failures. Let's embrace them as part of figuring it all out and as part of doing it all imperfectly. Let's take the pressure of time off and know that our goals are still valid even if they take a while to come to fruition.

We are all doing this imperfectly, in our unique and brilliant way.

Before I end this chapter, let me ask you a question: *what are you putting off out of fear of failure?*

Journal on that question (there's a whole chapter coming on journaling if you're new to it), talk it out to a trusted friend or mentor, or take a few minutes to meditate on the question.

If there's something that comes to mind, and failure is the *only* reason you're putting it off, know that it's probably something you need to do.

CHAPTER 6: ON BEING VISIBLE, HONEST, AND ALWAYS SCARED

My journey with visibility is at the heart of learning to love, own and honour my whole self and my quiet ambition.

Note: Before diving into this chapter on visibility, know that being visible in your business is not just about showing your face (although that can be part of it). It also means sharing your voice, taking up space with your words, being yourself in your content, bringing your personality into your brand, and sharing what's true to you.

New motherhood was the biggest shock of my life. I had no idea what it meant to be there for another person 100% of the time. I found it extremely difficult, and constantly wondered if I had made a huge mistake (which is hard to admit). But being shaken up in so many ways was an incredible catalyst for change in my life and business.

I want my son to grow up being proud of me. I want to be the example to him of someone doing what they are meant to do in the world, speaking about what they feel is important, and having the courage to put themselves out there in the name of the bigger vision.

Which is why – as you know – in June 2018 I decided to create my new Instagram account and finally start showing my face. Despite having had an online business for 10 years by this point, I had never put myself out there in this way and I had never been interviewed on a podcast (despite having been invited).

I told myself that my decision to stay hidden was because I was an introvert. I was also earning good money and didn't *need* to stretch my comfort zone. But the truth was that it was a decision purely based on fear and unchallenged decisions and beliefs about myself.

On the surface I didn't believe I was good enough, that I had anything worth saying, that anyone would want to listen, or that I was "the right kind of person" to share my voice more boldly. And yet, deep down, I felt "the nudge".

"The nudge" is what I call the inner knowing that you're meant to do something. It's not always rational, it doesn't always match up with those surface beliefs, but it keeps speaking to you underneath the layers of fear.

It didn't make sense for me to want to start speaking on video when it caused me so much anxiety. It didn't make sense for me to want to interview others on my podcast when I was socially awkward and shy. Why, on the one hand, did I want to completely hide away and, on the other hand, want to run this very visible online business through which I publish a blog, podcast, and books?

The more I've worked on it, the more I realise that the part of me that wants to hide away is not my true self. It's the fear, it's the social conditioning, it's small things that happened in my life that have made me think it's safer to hide away and dangerous to show my true personality and share my true feelings.

I have so much compassion for this fearful part of myself. After all, she is trying to protect me from repeating past hurts, and exposing myself to judgement, failure, or conflict with others. These are all real and valid psychological risks that may prevent us from wanting to get visible.

There's also a story – especially prevalent in introverts who are more naturally private people – that wanting to put yourself out there and be seen is narcissistic. There is nothing narcissistic about wanting to do what you were meant to do in this world. And there is nothing wrong with craving connection with likeminded humans – in fact, it's crucial to our confidence and happiness that we feel a sense of belonging. In my experience, learning to be all of yourself is how we get there (and in Chapter 8 I'll cover more about those times when we're *really* struggling to believe we're doing it right or that any of it is working).

Finding My Voice (One Instagram Story At A Time)

So back to June 2018, when I decided enough was enough, and I went all in[17]. I was bloody terrified, but I created my brand new Instagram account (though I'd had a previous "lurker" account for years) and started showing my face on Stories. I felt safer there, knowing that they would disappear within 24 hours. I also didn't have many followers, so in that sense it was easier to be visible because I knew there weren't many people reading and watching anyway!

---

[17] The biggest catalyst for change was my son, but I also need to give a shoutout here to the brilliant Ray Dodd (https://www.raydodd.co.uk) who was running a visibility course at the time, and Sara Tasker's Insta Retreat (https://meandorla.co.uk). Both of those courses gave me the accountability I needed to put my money where my mouth was.

The practice of recording a story, watching it back, and then doing it all over again has taught me so much. I doubted myself often, I would watch myself back and cringe, but eventually something started to shift. I started to get used to seeing my face and hearing my voice. Sometimes I'd watch back what I *thought* was me talking rubbish, only to hear that – just maybe – I actually had something good to say.

What helped was to ask myself what I find most interesting about other people and what they share online. Seeing the human behind the brand makes a difference, hearing someone's voice makes a difference, and being brought into small, everyday moments of other people's lives helps you to get to know them on a different level.

So I took how I felt about others and started to apply it to myself. I didn't fully believe it at first – but that's the way all beliefs get to change, by taking small action after small action, in alignment with the way you *want* to think and feel. And it shifted something for me.

I don't always feel like being visible (and I'll share more about boundaries and wanting to hide away a little later), and there's always a new level – like sharing my words in this book! What has always supported me is knowing that there is momentum in taking small steps close together. My mantra has always been to *keep on keeping on*.

I'll say it again: the only way to overcome a fear or change a belief is by taking action in alignment with how you want to feel, because that's what gives your brain the evidence that it is safe to do things differently than you've done before.

Once I had that evidence that it was safe to do things differently, I stretched my limits in wonderful ways that I never would have thought possible. I had "the nudge" to start a podcast (and I'll share more about what I mean by "the nudge" in Chapter 7 on journalling), and though I initially dismissed it as something that wasn't for "someone like me", building up evidence that I could be visible in those 15-second Story clips changed what I thought was possible.

I did it afraid, probably more afraid than the average human, and it turned out I was good at it. Getting uncomfortable and putting myself out there in new ways has been the best decision. The thing with comfort zones is that they stretch. Each time I tried something new I expanded what I believed I could do, and the impact this has had on my life and business has been incredible.

I am still scared all the time, I second-guess myself all the time, I cringe at myself and have moments where I wonder whether anything I'm saying is good enough. But facing the fear and discomfort is the best and hardest thing about this work. Even though putting yourself out there can bring up all of the feelings, even though this journey can feel incredibly hard, even though we may want to give up along the way... it is an incredible privilege to get to dig into our deepest darkest fears through the medium of business. To unravel the limiting decisions we have made about ourselves and to write a new story – one filled with possibility, self-compassion and acceptance.

Being Yourself Is Good For Business

Like I said at the beginning of this chapter, I don't believe that visibility has to look the same for everyone. You don't *ever* have to go on Stories, for example, to build a deeper connection with your people. And, for some business owners who aren't the "face" of their brand, it doesn't necessarily make strategic sense.

This chapter isn't about Instagram Stories specifically. It's about being ready and willing to let people see a little more of *you*. Why does that matter?

- When I show my face, when I share things that I'm struggling with, that's when I get messages. That's when I get replies. That's when I get to know people on a deeper level too because we have an exchange of conversation.
- When I do it imperfectly I save so much time. And going live is an amazing shortcut for being willing to show up imperfectly, teach people in the moment and receive real-time feedback.
- I am also so much more likely to buy things from the people who have a face, who have a voice, who are real, and fully rounded people in my mind compared to faceless companies.
- This is what makes showing your face, and recording video and/ or audio content a real "shortcut" for the growth of your business (though it's not for everyone, and there are plenty who are visible through their written words only).
- I'm much more likely to learn from someone who's being honest about how they started something and struggled with it as opposed to someone who's telling me: "here's how to do the thing in ten steps."
- It makes so much difference when people share their journey, their stories, their struggles, their values.

All of this comes down to being visible in a way that lets your personality show.

You Set The Rules

Most of my email subscribers and Instagram followers would probably tell you that I share quite openly with them. The truth is, I only share a small fraction of my life online.

As an introvert, I'm naturally inclined to share less, and it has been part of my journey to lean into sharing some of the more "mundane" parts of my life, trusting that people actually want to see it (and let's face it, I *do* live a pretty boring, simple life). But it's about more than introversion.

We do not owe our followers or subscribers anything. And being your true self never means sharing *all* of yourself.

Over time I decided that I wouldn't share much of my son, for example, or talk about my husband and family. I don't share much of my home, and, if I'm out and about, I have a rule never to post where I am until I've moved on to somewhere else.

I also recognise that, however fun it may be to share online, it can also take time away from me living my life. So I purposely take days, weeks and months away from social media when I feel I need it. As my business and audience has grown, the more I have felt confident not to share all the time (which, by the way, is a choice you can make no matter what your audience size).

My energy matters, too. My desire to be visible often ebbs and flows with my menstrual cycle (and side note: if you have periods, I highly recommend tracking for yourself the times *you* feel most chatty[18]). I tend to withdraw more in the "autumn" and "winter" phases of my

---

[18] Read the book *Period Power* by Maisie Hill for a comprehensive but easy-to-read guide to living in harmony with your cycle.

cycle, feeling the pull to be more visible during the "spring" and "summer".

And then there are times when I just reach my capacity. Sometimes I can predict when it'll happen (for example, after running a very visible 5-day live challenge), and sometimes it hits me without warning. The longer I do this, the less it takes me by surprise. But I want to normalise the fact that – whether introverted or not – we all crash and need to disappear sometimes. Be kind to yourself, don't beat yourself up for pushing too hard, but take it as an opportunity to learn a little more about the way you like to work and show up online.

Remember that you get to do this your way. Momentum helps, yes, so I encourage you to keep practicing. But know that consistency for solopreneurs is a myth. We are a human beings, and we all have our individual "sweet spot" and natural boundaries.

Forcing yourself to get on video just because everyone else is doing it is not a good reason to do it. What is a good reason is that tiny voice inside you that still wants to talk about it, despite the fear, that tells you *I can't not do this*. That is the only voice worth listening to. And believe me when I say, you are so much more comfortable than you think. Comfort zones can and will stretch the more you practice.

Showing Up Through Self-Doubt

Finally, let's talk about how self-doubt can make it hard to keep showing up. There are times when we need to take breaks from being visible (which I'll talk more about in chapters 11 & 12), and there are times when we *think* we need to take breaks because our self-doubt is telling us that what we're doing is (a) not good enough or (b) not safe to share.

All business owners have self-doubt, to some degree. For some, it manifests as a desire to prove ourselves by doing more (hello, overachievers). For others, it looks like freezing, procrastinating or finding "logical" ways to delay. And some of us will constantly prioritise the needs of others, or blame other things going on in our lives as reasons why we can't show up.

Whichever way self-doubt manifests in how you are visible, firstly show yourself some compassion. After having worked with hundreds of clients through these difficult feelings, and interviewed many brilliant humans for my podcast, I haven't yet met someone who hasn't doubted themselves at some point (and had it manifest in the ways described above).

When I was getting ready to launch my *Quietly Ambitious* podcast, I started to lose faith in my message and what I was doing. It felt very hard to show up and record episodes, and I struggled to believe that anything I was doing was good enough. Thankfully I was able to recognise this as a manifestation of self-doubt – it was simply rearing its head in response to stretching my comfort zone. I shared this experience with founder of the Self-Belief Coaching Academy, Sas Petherick, in episode #29 of the podcast[19], who reassured us all that it's totally normal, when trying new things, for self-doubt to crop up to try and protect you from the possibility that those new things go wrong.

You can gain awareness of the ways in which self-doubt shows up for you personally through coaching, and uncovering and healing the root causes of your self-doubt is a big part of the work I do. On a

---

[19] Listen to the full interview with Sas Petherick here: https://ruthpoundwhite.com/29-sas-petherick-on-redefining-leadership-self-compassion-the-archetypes-of-self-doubt/

personal level, being coached was transformational on my own self-belief journey – as was being surrounded by likeminded humans who shared openly about their own self-doubt. (My journalling practice has also been instrumental in creating new, more positive beliefs about myself, which I'll share in in the next chapter, and we'll talk more about creating more empowering meanings in Chapter 8).

Comments, testimonials, praise from others is all helpful in giving us evidence that what we're doing matters, and that we're doing a good job. But healing ultimately happens when we can trust in what we're doing and how we're showing up without the need for external validation (which is, by the way, a journey more than a destination most of us will reach 100% of the time – we are human, after all).

The best advice I can give you is to be visible and show up *even though* you doubt yourself. You have nothing to prove, to yourself or anybody else, but you have everything to gain from building momentum. And momentum comes from imperfect experimentation. Showing up, being your messy, imperfect self, making mistakes, learning and getting better over time.

I read some of the best advice about visibility in the book *Chillpreneur: The New Rules for Creating Success, Freedom, and Abundance on Your Terms* by Denise Duffield Thomas. The book is all about running your business in a way that works for you, that isn't stressful, and that ultimately makes your life easier (and Denise also happens to be the perfect example of an introvert running her business in a way that honours who she is). What she wrote about visibility stopped me in my tracks:

"I'm a contributor, not a guru. As soon as I gave myself permission to contribute to the conversation of women and money, and not have to be a guru or expert, then my business became fun.

If you really care about a topic, be a contributor. Who cares if you don't know everything? You don't have to be the best to make a difference to someone." – Denise Duffield-Thomas, *Chillpreneur*

If you're a contributor, you don't have to have all the answers. You don't need to be perfect. It's okay if you're learning and growing as you go. It's ok if you don't have the "best" ideas. Your audience is also going to be learning and growing with you at the same time.

Running your own business, putting your work into the world, and sharing your ideas with the world is fulfilling but it is never easy. The more you learn about how self-doubt shows up for you, the more you show up *even though* you're scared, the easier it gets to trust that you are safe to be all of you in your life and business.

Keep doing what you're doing because your work really does matter.

CHAPTER 7: JOURNALLING FOR BUSINESS OWNERS

Journalling is something I've done regularly in some form since I was a child.

My journalling practice started out as a daily diary. Now, it serves as a space to unload my thoughts, to process my feelings, to show myself compassion, to make faster decisions, to manifest my desires, to access my intuition and to focus on what matters to me.

There are so many ways to journal, and – as with everything included in this book – there is no One Right Way to journal. But throughout this chapter I'll share *my* way (including some of my most powerful prompts).

Why Journal?

Research suggests that journaling has multiple benefits for our well-being. Numerous studies have been conducted in different groups of people suggesting that journalling can reduce anxiety and depression, and may be as helpful as cognitive behavioural therapy. A 2020 study published in the *Archives of Psychiatric Nursing* found that "implementing a positive writing intervention is a practical means of promoting psychological well-being as a self-care strategy" for mothers of troubled children.[20]

Even better when your journalling practice includes some form of gratitude, which is consistently associated with greater happiness and mental wellbeing. In a study where participants were asked to write a few sentences per week either focusing on things that made them grateful (vs things that irritated them), the results after 10 weeks were that "those who wrote about gratitude were more optimistic and felt better about their lives. Surprisingly, they also exercised more and had fewer visits to physicians than those who focused on sources of aggravation." [21]

Personally, the practice of freewriting or Morning Pages (see below) can feel meditative. There are similarities in the way I feel after I meditate and after I journal. Mindfulness is the practice of being aware of your thoughts, and learning how to witness them without judgement. Both journalling and meditation have helped me to practice this skill. The difference is that journalling can (sometimes, not always) involve more space to explore the thought and ask what could be behind it.

Over time, patterns and themes may start to emerge from your journalling practice. A few years ago I was practicing a 2 minute daily

---

[20] See https://www.sciencedirect.com/science/article/abs/pii/S0883941720300078

[21] See https://www.health.harvard.edu/healthbeat/giving-thanks-can-make-you-happier

journalling check-in where I'd ask myself what went well about the day. After a few weeks I realised that I almost always judged how well my day had gone by how productive I had been. After noticing that pattern, I deliberately looked for other measures of "success", for example honouring my need to rest, being with my own feelings or getting outside and watching the bees visit the flowers in my garden.

From a business perspective, journalling is fantastic for building momentum. When you run a business on your own, you are responsible for every single decision. There are so many things we could be doing, so many different ways to run a business, and so much noise out there about which is the "best" that it makes sense for us to spin our wheels in overwhelm, not knowing what to do next. It's all completely normal human behaviour (especially for sensitive, overthinking humans!), but journalling about what you're afraid of is a great way to get back to momentum, and getting on with the work of actually building your business, not just thinking about it.

There are also times when you aren't sure what to say next in your content, or you're lacking in ideas for how to market your offer. By allowing yourself to just *write*, without editing your thoughts as you go, it can get the wheels turning for more to flow through. Sometimes, the journalling itself actually makes for content *gold* – many of my best emails and social media captions have come straight from my journal. The key, though, is not to journal as a means to an end. Most of what comes out in my journal will never see the light of day, and that's ok because it's all part of the process.

The Two Rules That Will Change Everything

Before we dive in to how I personally utilise this magical tool, there are two things I most want you to know about approaching journalling in this way...

Rule 1: You Cannot Get This Wrong

You CANNOT get this wrong, period. Whether you sit down for 5 minutes and write utter garbage (and, who's to judge it's garbage anyway?), or you sit down and write twenty pages of free-flowing brilliance, it's all subjective and it's the act of doing it that really counts.

Allow yourself to do this imperfectly, and to let your journalling practice evolve with you. You don't have to know exactly what you're doing; you don't have to be a great writer - you just have to do it.

I really hope that this goes some way to taking the pressure off this practice. Because I know that there are a lot of people shouting about how magical journalling can be (and they're right!), and that can lead to a perfectionist need to get it *just right* from the start. It is a process and a very individual journey. You can't get this wrong.

Rule 2: Journal From A Place of Self-Compassion

Journalling is and should always be **an act of self-love.** It is not another opportunity for you to beat yourself up over what you did or didn't do, or to stress about your to-do list. It is your sacred practice for connecting with your true self. And I can promise you this: your true self is worth listening to.

If you're new to journalling, or have a particularly loud "inner critic", then you may find that your journalling quickly sways towards the negative (mine certainly did a few years back). That's ok, don't beat yourself up about it - you are only human. However, please know that the negative voice isn't *all* of you. It is a *part* of you – I prefer to think of it as a "protective" part of you, there to help prevent you from psychological or physical harm (however misguided its protective language or behaviour may feel). But this voice is not *all* of you. There is so much more worth listening to if you have the tools to hear it.

I get that this isn't always as easy to access as I've made it sound, and I actually have some specific prompts to help you work with this. The first step, though, is simply noticing when your inner critic shows up in your journalling. As frustrating as it may feel when it does, awareness that it is happening is an incredible thing. Over time, it'll be easier and easier to let your highest, most true self do all of the talking.

And if you're protesting as you read this and thinking *but my inner critic needs listening to, or else how will I ever improve?* I get it. This critical voice is there to keep us safe in our comfort zone. Our true self is totally open to improvement, to stretching ourselves in the name of the highest vision we hold for our lives and businesses.

Freewriting and Morning Pages

The practice that really kickstarted my journalling habit was a form of freewriting – which simply means putting pen to paper and writing out whatever enters your mind in that moment.

I was introduced to this style of writing in the book *The Artist's Way: A Spiritual Path to Higher Creativity* by Julia Cameron, which I read in 2008 after graduating from university. I couldn't find a job, had all this free time on my hands, and was drawn to this method of accessing your creativity and letting go of blocks. So I gave the "Morning Pages" exercise a go.

The Morning Pages exercise requires you to write three pages in your journal, every single day when you wake up. You're not writing anything that you're going to use in any finished way – you're freewriting and the likelihood is that you'll never re-read those pages.

Does freewriting sound dauting to you? It's natural to have resistance, but the beauty of this practice is that if you can't think of anything to write, you simply write 'I can't think of anything to write.' In practice, if you can get used to switching off your "inner editor" for a few minutes, you'll find that you have more to write than you think. I would write down how I was feeling, what I had to do that day, how the weather was making me feel, ideas I had. It didn't have to be coherent or well written, it simply had to come out of my brain and onto the page via my pen (in fact, the pen often feels like it's moving itself without engaging my brain).

When writing Morning Pages, there's no specific goal in mind, you're letting the words spill out without pausing, and you keep going until you fill three pages. Those are the only rules. The beauty of doing this is the process itself, not the result. All that matters is that you write your thoughts, and no one else is ever going to read them.

An Alternative to Traditional Morning Pages

Although I love using pen and paper for journalling (it helps me access a different brain state), for a period of time I used a website called 750Words.com. It encourages you to stick to your Morning Pages every day by giving you a gamified version, including little badges for how many days you've written, statistics about how much you've written, how quickly you've written, and other metrics.

Using 750Words.com really encouraged my practice because I wanted to build up a streak, and avoid breaking that streak at all times. The time statistic also showed me how quickly I could do it and sometimes showed me how distracted I was.

Six Other Types of Journalling

Morning Pages was how I started, but I fell in and out of the habit, over time finding that there was a lot more to journalling. I now pick and choose how I do it depending on how I feel and what I am most drawn to in any given moment.

Here are some of the other types of journalling I have in my toolbox (and know that this is by no means an exhaustive list):

(1) Daily check-ins. One of my simplest and most powerful practices is to use a daily journalling check-in as part of a morning routine. Spending a few minutes to set an intention for how you want to feel that day can really make a difference to how the day plays out, and I'll share some specific exercises with you later in this chapter.

(2) Prompts. Unlike freewriting, using journalling prompts gives you a more defined starting point for your writing session. They're often in the form of a question which you can answer in your writing (though it's totally normal for one question to lead to *many* others, and that's ok). I'll share some prompts with you later on in this chapter.

(3) Affirmations. Affirmations are positive statements designed to impact our thought patterns. They are useful for helping us reprogramme specific limiting beliefs. For example, if you often think *I am not good enough at what I do* you can create an affirmation based on that statement to help you really accept that it's not true, for example: *I am enough,* and practice writing these out in your journal daily to help them sink in, or to remind you to take action in alignment with these chosen beliefs.

(4) Gratitudes. Keeping a gratitude journal, or including gratitudes as part of another journalling practice, is another way to reprogram the way you think. It is an opportunity to list everything good in your life, big or small. Some people find this easier than others, but you'd be surprised at how good it feels even to list the tiny things like *having a roof over my head*, or *getting an early night last night*.

(5) Scripting. Scripting is a form of manifestation in the law of attraction, where you write down your dreams and desires – things you want to bring into your reality – as if they have already happened. Whether you believe in the law of attraction or not, this can be a powerful exercise in getting clearer on your goals, and feeling into why they matter to you.

(6) Asking yourself questions & writing to your intuition. If you're stuck on anything in life, then you can journal on the question. Simple questions like *which path should I choose?* or *why can't I come up with a solution for this problem?* can be incredibly powerful in uncovering ideas or things going on in your mind that you aren't consciously aware of (there really is something magical about putting pen to paper when you're stuck on something).

Accessing Your Inner Wisdom (Or Intuition) Through Your Journal

I wholeheartedly believe that trusting in yourself is a superpower in business.

Over time, and with practice, through my journal I learned to access the part of me that knows the truth. Call it intuition, source, higher self, sovereign, core... this is the part of me that has made incredible things happen in my life and business, once I learned how to listen to it.

Episode #25 of *the Anthill* podcast featured interviews with several psychologists on the science behind intuition[22]. In short, studies have shown that our brains make snap decisions and reactions based on subconscious judging against historical situations that we've been in. This is what we call a "gut feeling" - and it's based on subtle cues that your conscious brain hasn't had time to fully process yet. For this reason, our gut feelings work best in situations where we have more experience. There's more history to compare it to.

Intuition kicks in most often when you either have too much information or not enough. It's a way of keeping us calm in the midst of chaos or danger. So it makes sense to me that it can be a useful tool for business owners (particularly the sensitive ones).

As entrepreneurs there are so many possible paths for us to take, and so much information to take in. Overwhelm is a common stumbling block, but our intuition can help drown out the noise, keep us focused, and help us move forward. You know your business better than anyone, so use your intuition as a way to let go of the "shoulds" and prioritise what's right for you.

Your intuition also matters because it's directly related to the way you feel. And how you feel about your work directly impacts how good you feel about life in general. How good you feel impacts your energy. How good you feel impacts how good you are at what you do. How good

---

[22] See https://theconversation.com/anthill-25-intuition-96677

you feel impacts how others feel when working with you. Most importantly, how good you feel impacts your quality of life - and that matters.

Not to mention that certain business strategies and marketing tactics can feel better than others (especially for sensitive business owners, who may find it hard to follow all the "rules"). Intuition can also help us discern between an action or decision that is right for us as individuals, vs one that we think we "should" make because we've heard it from someone else. And when you feel good about the way you are working and what you're putting out there, it's far easier to find the energy to sell what you're doing (and to let them share in your own excitement about your work).

Our intuition isn't infallible. It gets stronger and stronger the more experience you have in a given area, so it's expected - and totally ok - that you'll make mistakes sometimes. As a business owner, mistakes are never *really* mistakes, though. Everything you try and "fail" at will provide useful information going forward.

Trusting your intuition also doesn't mean you don't have things to learn or that you can't be supported by experts and coaches. You absolutely can! But definitely do use your intuition when deciding who it is that you want to work with.

It's important to note here that intuition is also influenced by cognitive bias: when we follow ideas just because lots of other people think something (hello patriarchy and white supremacy! I see you). This is why it's so important to take off the layers of who we are while also learning to trust what we think. And remember - mistakes are a huge part of the journey towards building a successful business, and especially in building one that feels good and right to you.

Building Your Intuitive Muscle Through Journalling

When you're not used to using your intuition, it can be hard to even hear that inner knowing. A lifetime of social conditioning, and a long social media feed full of other people's opinions, can massively drown out that inner wisdom. That's why I recommend using a number of exercises and journal prompts to teach you how to tune into this powerful part of yourself.

Step 1 is always to give yourself the time to just sit and be quiet. We can't hear when it's too noisy. So give yourself moments to pause and breathe throughout the day. Perhaps try a grounding meditation[23], go sit in the sunshine, or lie down for 5 minutes without any music or podcasts playing. Whatever works for you!

Next, experiment with easy decisions that don't have too many consequences, things like 'does my intuition want me to wear the blue top or the yellow top?' or going on a walk and changing direction based on what your intuition tells you to do.

Know that it's totally normal if this feels a little bit difficult or weird at first. That's ok. You've probably had a lifetime of cultural conditioning telling you not to trust your gut feelings, to look to what others are doing to make your own decisions, and to base decisions on results rather than feelings. Just know that it gets easier, especially if you view it as a fun experiment.

---

[23] My Journalling for Business Owners course includes a pre-writing meditation: https://ruthpoundwhite.com/journal/

Once you've started practicing following your intuition, there are many exercises you can use to build that intuitive muscle. I've included a detailed list in my free guide, *The Art of Aligned Action-Taking & How to Listen To Your Intuition in Business*.[24] For the purposes of this chapter, let's stick to journalling with some specific prompts that can get us in touch with our highest self.

Three Powerful Journal Prompts for Accessing Your Intuition & Getting to Know Yourself Better

Choose a prompt based on what feels good to you in this moment. Have a glance over them all and pick the one that feels right. Remember, this takes practice and may not always come easily – just remember the 2 key rules from earlier in this chapter: know that you cannot get this wrong, and journal from a place of self-compassion.

(1) What does my heart want to say today? *Write freely without judging what comes up. This is how you learn to tap into your heart instead of your mind (which is often clouded by doubt and fear).*

(2) What do I need to know right now? *This question is the perfect way of tapping in with your higher self - that wise inner version of you who isn't afraid, who is open to new opportunities, and who knows they already have everything they need within them.*

(3) [If you have a specific question that needs answering]

---

[24] Download the free bundle of guides & workbooks here: https://ruthpound.lpages.co/aligned-action-taking-freebie/

Write down your question in your journal, close your eyes and take 5 deep breaths in and out, then open your journal and freewrite. Let whatever wants to come up, come up. Remember, all the answers are already inside you.

Use the following prompts to tap into all areas of inner knowing. Simply start your journal entry with the words in the prompt, and let the words flow freely (without judging what's coming up).

- I am...
- I want...
- I feel...
- I'm ready for...
- I let go of...

How to Use Journalling Specifically for Your Business

If you make use of everything I've already shared in this chapter, your business will benefit. You will support yourself to feel better, to access brilliant ideas that come straight from your intuition, and to build greater momentum by making faster decisions.

Before we finish I want to offer you the most powerful advice for journalling as a business owner: get into the habit of being curious about your thoughts, feelings and actions, and ask yourself questions in your journal about what's going on.

For example, perhaps you notice yourself resisting working on a certain project. Being curious about this behaviour means not beating yourself up for it (after all, we all experience these feelings sometimes), but asking yourself what it might be trying to tell you. Use that question as a starting point for your journalling session: *'what is this resistance trying to tell me right now?'* or *'why am I resisting this specific project?'*

When you start writing, don't search for the 'logical' answer. Just write. Write down how it makes you feel, write down what the consequences of your action – or in-action – might be. Write down whatever pops into your mind. The more you practice, the easier it gets, and you'll eventually find that journalling makes it far easier to understand what's going on than thinking alone.

Journalling is also helpful for exploring difficult feelings. When you're doubting that what you're doing is good enough, when you're launching but you fear it won't sell, or when you're worried about whether you're cut out for any it... journal about it. Ask yourself why this matters to you, why you started this in the first place, where you've surprised yourself in the past in terms of what you were capable of, and how you can lean into trust in the present. If you need to, simply list out all the things you're afraid of without asking anything else of yourself. I promise that you will feel better able to move forward when you've done so.

Journalling is the practice that will teach you curiosity and self-compassion in the place of self-criticism and staying stuck in limiting thought patterns or beliefs. And before long you'll find that these skills translate to the way you think in the moment, too.

I hope that that this chapter has encouraged you to try journalling for your business and for yourself. And I have several free and paid journalling resources if you need more guidance or themed prompts:

1. Download the free *Art of Aligned Action-Taking & How to Listen To Your Intuition in Business* guides & workbooks here - https://ruthpound.lpages.co/aligned-action-taking-freebie/
2. Sign up for my **seven-day journalling challenge** to get you into the habit of journalling every day for a week (including a collection of prompts) at journalweekchallenge.com
3. Sign up to my **8-part Journalling for Business Owners course**, which teaches you everything you need to know to create your own powerful ritual (plus meditations and prompts) at https://ruthpoundwhite.com/journal/
4. Or sign up to my **Journalling for Launches** course to learn how to really get behind your offer energetically, managing your energy and unravelling "stories" throughout the launch, and what to learn from afterwards - https://ruthpoundwhite.com/o/launchjournal
5. Finally, gain the confidence to show up in your business and make more money with **a year's worth of prompts** that help you unpack the things that are limiting you - https://ruthpoundwhite.com/year-of-prompts/

CHAPTER 8: HOW TO KEEP SHOWING UP (EVEN WHEN IT'S HARD)

Think of this chapter as the heart of this book. It's about how to keep showing up for your business and yourself, even when you're struggling, even when you doubt yourself, even when it feels like it's not working, that you're not "succeeding", or that it's all "too much".

Keep showing up is a guiding mantra for me in my business.

It helped me when I was starting out and wondered whether anything was working for me, if it was worth all the effort.

Keep showing up.

It helped me to remember that this is all about the long game of consistently putting myself and my work out there out there, even when I didn't know exactly how and when it would all pay off.

Keep showing up, even when it's hard.

In this chapter I'll share with you what it means to *really* trust in the work you are doing, what it takes to build the resilience you need to make it all pay off, how to work through the stories that your brain gives you to try to keep you safe, and what it really takes to build momentum. (Chapter 11, on the other hand, is all about maintaining your energy and honouring your natural cycles and need to rest).

One Day You'll Look Back And It'll All Make Sense

I had a big advantage when I started my second business: I already knew what it was like to start something from scratch and to have to wait for it all to come to fruition and make sense. As you know, I ran my first business for over ten years, and there came a point where it all finally felt like a "success" and made sense in hindsight: all of the struggle, all of the working for little pay in the early days, and all of the mistakes.

On the other hand, thanks to starting all over again with my coaching business in 2019, I also remember how it feels to be in those earlier stages of wondering where it's all going and whether you'll ever figure it out at all. I know both stages of the business journey well.

All business owners know that they need to show up, do the work, and get their offers in front of their right people for it all to take off. But that doesn't mean it's easy to keep doing it. You are going to have setbacks and challenges, I guarantee it. It's how you deal with those setbacks that can make or break your business (and your sanity).

Showing up isn't all about showing your face or being visible every day, on every platform. It's about carrying on doing the work with some faith that you're actually doing ok, that it all matters, and that you are going to get well compensated for it.

It's so easy in the early days to take small setbacks as a sign you're on the wrong track. But what happens when you constantly question it? You spin your wheels, you move from one thing to the next without giving anything a proper chance, and you send mixed messages to your audience about what you're really here to offer. Or you have a launch flop and throw out the whole offer, instead of tweaking your messaging, and trying again.

All of this behaviour is completely normal, by the way. Whenever we're doing something we haven't done before, our brain will try to keep us safe by looking for the evidence that it's working. And changing your strategy in some way – whether that means trying lots of new things or even stalling and disappearing for a while – will feel safer than sitting with the unknown.

The *only* way you'll get to the point where it all works out for you is to keep showing up, but it requires resiliency. And I promise you will build the resiliency required of you as a business owner the more you keep showing up, even when it's hard.

What I most need you to know is that **your business is going to work in the way you want it to,** even if it doesn't feel like it right now, *as long as you keep going.*

One day you will look back in hindsight and see that every single piece of work you have done has contributed to who you have become and what you have created. Every setback will have taught you a lesson. Every failed launch will have taught you something about how to do it better next time, every time your content gets seen by a tiny fraction of your audience will teach you something about using your voice by the time that audience grows, every single sale you make – even if it doesn't meet your goals – is a stepping stone in the right direction.

When I look back at my journey, I am so grateful to 21-year-old-me, who started even though she didn't know what she was doing, who persevered even when she could barely pay the rent, who never gave up because she knew she didn't want to get a "real job". Even though that version of me wasn't yet ready to show herself and speak her truth, she was willing to experiment, to play around, to learn new skills.

Now when I look back, I can tell that all of those hours I put in unpaid were totally worth it. You're not going to know that if you're in the earliest stages of your business or if you've been doing this for a few months or even a few years. You're not going to know how all the work that you're doing now is going to pay off in future.

And that is why showing up is, at the core, about having faith before you have the evidence, and trusting in the momentum that is building under the surface.

Remember When You Wanted What You Currently Have?

For those of you who aren't brand new but still have a feeling that you should be doing "better" by now, it's helpful to remember when you wanted what you currently have.

The negativity bias means that humans are far more likely to take on the weight of something negative, even if presented alongside something positive of equal significance. What this means for our businesses is that we need to make a conscious effort to look for what's actually working, not just what isn't.

In my coaching & mentoring business, £5K months were the goal for a long time, and they felt so out of reach. At some point, I celebrated my first £5K month, and £5K months started feeling completely normal. I was so focused on the next goal of £10K months that I had to actually remind myself to appreciate how far I had come. There's always a next level that we're working towards, but you have so much progress to celebrate *now* (which is why I am always asking my 1:1 and group clients to celebrate their wins, big and small – and often).

Don't forget that financial milestones aren't the only ones worth celebrating. The milestones include the people you impact along the way, learning what you *don't* want your business to look like, the difficult situations that come along and teach you how to better deal with the next level of your business.

In the early days of my second business, I was bringing in very little, but I had been releasing weekly podcast episodes for a few months. My coach at the time, Ray Dodd, asked me how else I could define success beyond finances. I thought about all the comments and messages I had about my work, the people who told me it gave them permission to be more of who they were, and I realised I was already making an incredible impact with my work (even if I wasn't - yet - getting well paid for it).

My job as a coach now is to remind you of what's so easily forgotten in our most vulnerable moments. That question from my own coach encouraged me to keep going when I wasn't yet seeing all the fruits of my labour. And in the keeping going, I've built a business and life that I am very proud of (financially and otherwise).

Celebration is a key part of keeping the momentum going. And momentum is *everything* when it comes to making it all happen.

Two Questions To Ask Yourself When It's Not Happening Quickly Enough

In my experience, the feeling of it not happening "quickly enough" is something that we come up against at all stages of business. Wanting to know whether it's all working in the beginning, wondering how and when it'll get easier, realising you have bigger and bigger goals, or new levels that you still want to reach. Your brain will look for the evidence that you're doing the right thing at every stage of the way.

Have you ever been in a car when a child keeps asking, every minute of the journey, *are we there yet*? I have, and I can tell you it makes that journey a whole lot less fun. When you ask yourself this question about your business, you take your energy away from more productive or joyful places, you stifle creativity, and it feels pretty crappy.

We're all human, so first have compassion for the fact that you feel this way. Then ask yourself – or your journal – these two important questions:

Question 1: "Am I doing this? Can I *not* do this?"

Meaning: *"Am I going to make this work no matter what?"; "Have I <u>decided</u> I'm making this work, even if I don't know how or when?"*

When I say no matter what, I don't mean at the expense of your health, happiness or relationships. What I really mean is trusting that eventually you're making it *all* work in harmony with those things: *"Have I decided I'm building my business in the way that I have chosen it to be?"*

If the answer is yes, then the question of how long it takes suddenly holds less weight. Because I've decided I'm doing it, which takes a lot of the second-guessing out of the equation.

You may also like to ask yourself this question from a different angle: *"Can I <u>not</u> do this?"* Whenever I ask myself this question, I know that there's no way I want to go out and get a regular job. This life and business I have chosen for myself is challenging and uncomfortable at times, but I know I can't *not* do it.

And if you *can* not do this, that's ok! Maybe there's an alternative route you can explore. Maybe there's a different career path, or maybe you can take the pressure off with a part-time job. Let the answer guide your next steps.

Question 2: "If I 100% knew this was happening, how would I now feel about the timing?"

Imagine the time in the future when it has all happened the way you're dreaming of now, you just don't know exactly when. How would that change how you currently feel about the timing in this moment? Would it still be not quick enough? Or would there be more acceptance that the journey is your journey?

It is natural and human to question the timing. We have fears that it won't work out the way we want, and we want the evidence now to prove to us that we're doing the right thing, and that it's safe to keep going. But at the same time, does part of you trust that the journey is your journey for a reason?

In my previous business I spent so long trying to get above barely bringing in minimum wage. When my income finally took off, I realised that I had learned so much that it all made sense. The foundations that had felt like such a slog to build at the time had now become the bedrock of my now successful business.

How Not To Take Everything in Business So Personally

I know, easier said than done, right?! But not taking things personally in my business has been a key part of why I've been able to make it work and build up the necessary momentum.

It's really easy to feel like you and your business are the same thing. How this can manifest (and don't worry if you do this, because most of us do) is, for example, putting something out there on social media, noticing it doesn't get the engagement you might have hoped for, and making it mean something about you personally.

Or it could also be putting an offer out there that was really aligned to how you want to be working and the transformation you want to facilitate for your people. You put your heart and soul into working on it, but then you don't get the signups that you wanted (or even needed for it to be viable). That then means that you aren't good enough as a business owner, as a person, that your work isn't good enough and just isn't resonating.

But we are not the same as our business. When we start making decisions from a place of looking for certain results to validate us, that's where things can get very, very tricky. Essentially what you're putting out there, the entire future of your business, what you decide to do and how you decide to run it all comes back to whether other people validate your idea.

But a key part of being an entrepreneur and growing a business is having a vision that is bigger than the current reality of what is happening in this moment. Can you see the problem?

At this point, you may be thinking: *hang on Ruth, but you do actually need people to validate what you do, because you need to make money from your business!* That's true. You need to put offers out there that people resonate with and make money in return, or else it's not a business.

But there is a difference between building that long term profitable business that makes the sales, has the customers, makes the profit etc. vs. making micro-decisions on a daily basis based on the engagement you get on social media, the numbers of replies you get to an email, or one random negative comment you received that day. There is an *important* difference, however subtle it may feel.

The Practice of Detaching (& Separating Emotions From Facts)

The difference comes from being willing and able to look at things from a detached point of view. When we put something out there, it doesn't get the response we were looking for, and we make it mean something about us – our value, our worth, our good-enough-ness (or lack of) - that is not detached. When you're entangling all of those things with your business, it makes it really hard to see clearly the things that you do have control of and can strategically improve, vs. the things that you can't control and/ or will keep you stuck.

Let's say you are running a free masterclass as a way to grow your audience and get a bit of buzz before you launch a paid product. You consider what you want to talk about, how you want to communicate the topic of that masterclass with your people, what you want to write on your signup page, and then you put your masterclass out there. People are clicking through to visit the page but only 10% of those people are actually signing up for this free offer.

At this stage you might, naturally, get upset and personally offended. *Why aren't these people signing up? I must not be good enough! Does anyone even like what I do? Am I doomed to fail in my business if I can't even promote something free? This is the story of my life, I'm just not good at any of this.*

You have a choice in how you respond here. We all feel like this sometimes, so have compassion for yourself when you do, and allow yourself to wallow for a bit if that's what you need. Ask yourself whether you choose to stay there, or whether anything else could be true?

The key questions are: "what about this situation is under my control?" "what can I potentially tweak?" and "how can I look at this differently?"

Using the masterclass as an example, this could have gone in two different directions. The first option – where you attach all of that meaning about the number of signups to how good you are at what you do – could leave you cancelling the masterclass, or completely changing the topic without thinking it properly through. Either way, you're not really giving yourself a chance to see what might work instead.

If you can detach, you might simply decide to change the headline on the landing page instead. You remind yourself it's a simple, practical element of the process that means nothing about you. You're simply making small changes, testing, tweaking, and giving it a little time to see what happens. Or maybe you decide to give it a different name, maybe you decide to format the landing page differently to make it all clearer.

Making small tweaks in the areas you can control is a lot more effective than going down the rabbit hole of questioning or throwing away everything you're doing (ask me how I know).

Sometimes you'll find that there are clear things that need to be tested, and sometimes it's not so clear cut. Sometimes you're in a launch, you've done all the work ahead of time, you've put your thing out there, but you're not seeing any evidence that anyone wants to sign up yet. Launching always brings up the fears and the feelings, even when you've still got time left to bring people in. *My work doesn't resonate! People don't like me or my offer! People don't have the money to spend, don't value what I do!*

As I share in detail in my Journalling for Launches course, the key questions to ask yourself in these moments are:[25]

1. What can I control in this situation? And what is a case of me trusting and waiting out?
2. What am I making this mean, and is this meaning 100% true?
3. What else could be true?

Maybe you'll realise that your launch is far from being the flop that you've begun to think it is. You can send another email, or follow up with specific people who haven't replied to you yet. And then you'll take some time to really look at your mindset in this moment, with questions like:

- *What am I really believing in this moment?* I'm believing that my offer isn't good enough.
- *What's that telling you believe?* I believe that I don't know how to market effectively.

---

[25] If you want the full process for working through these stories as they come up, then it is all detailed in my Journalling for Launches course: https://ruthpoundwhite.com/o/launchjournal

- *What's that telling you believe...* and keep digging down through the layers to get to the core, underlying belief, which in this case could be <u>I'm</u> *not good enough.*

And then get some coaching, do some journaling, do some exercises and ask yourself, what do I need to put into place, how do I actually want to feel instead, what thought or feeling is accessible for me to feel in this moment? For example, even though in this moment I feel not good enough, I am still able to access the feeling of "doing my best" (there's no need to act as if you believe *"I am completely amazing, and doing everything right",* because when it's so far from the truth your mind is probably going to reject that).

Then we get practice taking this thought out into reality. Ask yourself: *"if I really trusted that I was doing my best, what actions would I be taking in this launch right now?"* You'll be surprised at how this practice of detaching from the results, asking yourself the right questions and then acting in alignment with a different feeling or belief can lead to a very real difference in what happens next.[26]

What Else Could Be True?

If you take away just one thing from this chapter, let it be this question: *"what else could be true?"*

As I mentioned earlier, human beings have a very real negativity bias. As a way to keep ourselves safe, we notice the negative far more

---

[26] Note: This is part of "mindset recoding" work I do with my clients on a regular basis, if you want to find out more head to https://ruthpoundwhite.com/work-with-me/

easily than the positive, so that we can prepare and protect ourselves against any possible risk.

As business owners, we get to constantly remind ourselves that the risk of *not* doing the thing we want to do is far greater than the risk of potentially failing at it, or being judged by others. And we get to create new stories that support us to feel safer in the actions we are taking.

When we ask ourselves, "what else could be true?", we are more likely to see the situation for what it really is. For example, when nobody replies to an email you sent to your email list and you wonder if it resonated at all, what else could be true is simply that people are reading and enjoying it but not taking the time to reply (because replying to an email, after all, takes more effort than liking a post on social media).

Sometimes asking "what else could be true?" requires a little more digging and searching for the evidence that it's working. When you're struggling to sell out your 1:1 offer, look for the evidence that people are enjoying what you're sharing, that you're making an impact, and that they're reaching out even if they're not ready to work with you yet.

And just sometimes, asking "what else could be true?" means making up a much better story for yourself. Imagining the one person out there who is having a conversation with their partner about how to afford to work together, you just don't know it's happening. Or the people who have your signature course on their vision board. Or the people listening to your podcast saying to themselves "I'll work with her one day" (I remember thinking this of two of my own mentors, both of which took a while to materialise, and both of which had no idea I was "lurking" in their world until I finally reached out).

CHAPTER 9: OUR BUSINESSES CAN CHANGE THE WORLD

Of all the chapters in the book, this one makes me the most nervous. However, it would be doing you and me a disservice not to talk about the ways in which I believe that our businesses can change the world for the better.

As a heart-led entrepreneur, I need to believe that my work matters and that I'm contributing something to the world, no matter how small. I've tried to fight it – because it all feels pretty idealistic and potentially naïve – but it's how I'm wired.

It feels audacious. It even feels pretentious. Who are we to think that we can change the world? What does making a difference even mean? Yes, it's the celebrities and the billionaires donating to important causes and setting up foundations who are changing the world. It's the people on the streets leading protests for change who are making a difference. It's the doctors and the nurses and the teachers making a direct impact in their communities every single day... *but it's not only them.*

Aren't we also making a difference by sharing our mental health struggles and spreading awareness in our social media captions? Doesn't making a difference also include those of us who are unapologetically showing up as ourselves and inspiring others to do the same? Shouldn't we also give more credit to the small business owners who work tirelessly behind the scenes and without any fanfare to source eco-friendly materials or consciously choose to make their work more accessible, even when it decreases their profit margins?

Sometimes it's uncomfortable to believe that it's possible to make a difference, especially as one person, or as someone who may not have the same privileges as others, or who finds it difficult to use their voice. But, as the writer and feminist marketing consultant Kelly Diels says, "Tiny acts of doing it differently are culture-making."[27]

If we care about something and we want to do work in alignment with our values, then we are making a difference, even if we haven't yet figured out exactly how. We are remaking our culture in a way that is better for everyone. The more that we lean into the discomfort of claiming that, the more we empower others to do the same.

You Are Already Changing the World By Being You

I say it all the time: there are people out there who need what you're doing, exactly in the way you're doing it, with your unique combination of experience, philosophy, personality and way of communicating. You are the only one that can do the thing you do, in exactly the way you do it. This is what I mean by being "the right person for your right people".

What does this have to do with changing the world, I hear you ask? It's about reaching the people that only you can reach. Sharing your ideas in the way that only you can. Having a voice that matters because

---

[27] See the full article "Culture making = tiny acts of doing-it-differently" by Kelly Diels here: https://www.kellydiels.com/culture-making-means-tiny-acts-differently/

your right people need to hear it, and having an impact on those people that nobody else could match.

It doesn't mean that you're perfect at what you do, it means that your unique combination of experience, philosophy, personality, and way of communicating all comes together to be the perfect person for your perfect people.

Your right people need your fears, your doubts, and your failures too. I've had huge imposter syndrome about writing and publishing this book. I've wondered why I need to be the one to put this into the world. I am a massive introvert, writing about being a massive introvert who is terrified of each new level of visibility. And by being honest about this anxiety at each stage of the way, I have connected with so many humans who can now see what might be possible for them, too.

I don't have millions of readers, followers or podcast listeners. But my voice and my vulnerability are making a difference, because I share my experiences from the perspective of someone who understands who my right people are. That is the start of a beautiful ripple effect of influence.

In episode #36 of the *Quietly Ambitious* podcast[28], creative coach Nicola Rae Wickham shared that showing up as herself is a form of activism for her because, as a Black woman, she didn't see people like her doing things she dreamed of when she was growing up. Sometimes showing up as yourself – unapologetically – is enough to set new examples for people like you.

---

[28] Listen to the full conversation with Nicola Rae Wickham on episode #36 of the *Quietly Ambitious* podcast here: https://ruthpoundwhite.com/36-nicola-rae-wickham-on-showing-up-as-yourself-dreaming-big-affirmations-for-business-owners/

Personally I write about being an introverted, chronically tired and breadwinning business owner and mother. Again it feels audacious to claim that this is world-changing, but we need more people to share their experiences when they are outside of the societal norms.

On the flip side, *you don't have to share anything you don't want to share.* And I acknowledge that as a white cisgendered woman it is far safer for me to "be myself" than it may be for others. I have also had access to a good education, and I've always been brought up with the narrative that I could achieve whatever I wanted, so I'm starting from that point of privilege in my business. I'm not going to pretend that my privilege doesn't exist or that everything I have created in my business has been a result of me having a dream and making it happen because that's not true. There is a wider discussion needed about this privilege in the online business world.

Which is why I also believe that we have a responsibility to use our platforms and to think about whose voices we are amplifying alongside our own. We need to think about what we charge and how we spend our money to address the inequality in the world. We need to get outside of our bubbles of social media and what we normally read and listen to, and hear about other people's experiences.

"I raise up my voice - not so I can shout but so that those without a voice can be heard. We cannot succeed when half of us are held back."

– Malala Yousafzai.

Individual Acts Add Up to a Wider Network of Change

A few years ago I asked my Instagram followers to share with me how they are changing (or hoping to change) the world with their work. Their responses really highlighted how we're all doing this in our own way, and that we're all playing to our own individual strengths to help people that can most benefit from what we do.

I received answers from lots of coaches helping women recognise their potential, learn to believe in themselves and have happy, fulfilled lives. There were creative writers and artists helping people to better explore their inner worlds. There were shop owners making a stand against rapid consumption by taking a more slow and sustainable approach. And influencers creating entire platforms dedicated to amplifying the voices of people from marginalised groups.

When sharing their answers with me, many told me they found it hard to admit that they were changing the world, but that they were definitely trying to make an impact in their corner of the world for individuals and even for their own families through financial freedom. I get it, and it's why writing this chapter made me nervous in the first place. It sounds bold and big to think that we want to change the world. Who are we to claim that we're doing it? But in claiming it, we shine a light on the many and varied ways in which we get to do it.

After sharing several replies in my stories, one follower summed it up perfectly when she said that seeing everyone's messages had been a lovely reminder that **the little bits we are each doing are part of a wider network of individual acts that together have the power to change the world**.

It's clear from these examples – from a very small sample of my Instagram following – that changing the world can mean something different for everyone. What matters is that we (a) own the fact that we do want to change the world in our own small way and (b) stay connected to our purpose within the day to day running of our businesses.

Staying Connected To Your Bigger Purpose

Staying connected to the bigger purpose for why you do what you do not only helps you to stay true to your bigger mission in the world, and to make faster decisions (which in turn builds momentum more quickly) – it gives you an important reason to keep going when things feel hard, and you'll also notice that you start to believe more in the value of what you do and the possible legacy that you might create.

In his book *Company of One: Why Staying Small is the Next Big Thing for Business,* Paul Jarvis shared that studies on the biggest businesses have shown that companies with a strong purpose do better, outgrowing other companies that didn't have a strong purpose by 12%.

What I really want you to take away from this section is that, as easy as it can be to get bogged down in the day-to-day running of your business, it's important to take a step back to consider how you're working. Give yourself space to think about your fulfilment, what matters to you, the legacy you wish to leave, and how you can get well paid to do all of those things.

Journalling is the perfect tool for doing this. Aside from freewriting – which I regularly tune into to connect with why it all matters, and which we talked about in Chapter 7 – here are 5 different journalling-based exercises you can use now to tune into why it all matters (you don't need to do them all – pick the one that resonates right now).

Exercise 1: Journal On These Specific Prompts

Write a paragraph or two about why you do what you do. It doesn't have to be perfect, it simply has to feel true. It has to give you the tingles. And, as always, you can intuitively pick and choose journalling prompts and leave any behind if they don't feel right for you. Some examples:

- Why am I here?
- What was I born to do?
- What's my legacy?
- My vision for myself and my family is...
- My vision for my clients and community is...
- My vision for the wider world is...
- What role does money play in all of this?

If these questions feel big to look at, know that actually journalling on them - or speaking your answers out loud if you prefer - takes some of the weight out of them. Allow yourself to write whatever comes up, and know that is just right.

Exercise 2: The Five Whys

Start by asking yourself, *why am I in business?* Write out the answer in your journal. Then you ask yourself *why?* again, write out the answer, and keep asking *why?* until you've done it five times. By the time you get to the fifth answer, you should have the real, deepest reason why you're doing what you're doing.

Exercise 3: Write a Letter From Your Future Self

Sometimes it's easier to get big, bold and audacious about your legacy and impact when you tune into a future version of yourself, many years from now. Pick any time period in the future that comes to you intuitively. It could be one year or five years from now, or even you writing from your deathbed (a powerful exercise I learned from one of my own mentors, Suzy Ashworth). Write a letter to yourself about what you've achieved, how you've helped people in your business, what the ripple effect of that has been, and how it all feels.

Exercise 4: Get Specific About Your Offers & Services

Get a sheet of paper and split it into two columns. The first column is the more direct ways your offers and services help people, and the second column is the bold, perhaps less direct, the ripple effect.

For example, for my course "Clarify", the first column might have something like "help people save time and feel less stressed in their businesses" or "give people more mental space so that they can think about ways to change the world with their businesses", and the second column might be something massive, like, "give people greater capacity to heal" and the ripple effect this has on their children and on the world.

For a physical product the first column might include "helping people to create more beautiful homes" or "giving them happy post to look forward to", and the second column might include "improving mental health and happiness when their homes are a nicer place to be" or "inspiring other makers to live their dreams and start their own businesses."

In my experience asking clients to complete this exercise, this comes easier to some than it does to others. It can be hard to allow yourself to think that your small offer could have a world-changing impact, but the more you practice this the easier it gets.

Exercise 5: Uncover Your Core Business Values

Your core business values aren't fixed, they will change, and it's helpful to revisit this exercise once a year or so. I have an entire free workbook that takes you through the whole progress (you'll get it when you subscribe to my newsletter at https://ruthpoundwhite.com/newsletter/), so here's the short version:

1. Start by journalling on what matters most to you, and the moments in life when you've felt proudest.
2. Notice whether there are any themes, and write down words to represent these themes.
3. It can also be helpful to look at a list of values words (there are many out there on the internet) and pick your top 5-10.
4. Narrow it down to the ones that matter most to you, and you have your values.
5. Now journal on what each one of those words means to you personally and in your business, and ask yourself how you can embody them more in your work and life.

As an example, my top business value is freedom. I reached that conclusion from doing the exercise I shared with you above. I want everyone to be free to be who they really are, to express themselves, to run a business in a way that honours their mind and body, to be able to take time off to travel or to pursue other interests, and to have a wealth of choice when it comes to the way I spend my money. When I make business decisions, I regularly ask myself whether they are supporting my core value of freedom.

12 Practical Ways We Can Make A Difference As Sensitive Online Business Owners

Let's talk about some of the practical and real ways in which we can make a difference in the world as online business owners and creatives.

Starting with an important preface to this section: please don't make yourself anxious or overwhelmed about what you're *not* doing, or not doing perfectly.

There's always more to be done, and we can and should aim to do better when we know better. But there's a lot going on in the world, so much to be done in terms of social justice, the climate crisis, and other worthy causes. None of us can do everything, and for many of us the biggest impact we can have in these areas will be made indirectly, through tiny acts of doing things differently in our own corner of the world.

Many of us – especially women – already have a huge mental load to carry, and wanting to make a difference can sometimes feel like a burden. In the past I've found myself overwhelmed by simple choices of which products to use in my household, or which food to buy. It's all worth thinking about, but not to carry so much guilt and responsibility that it affects my mental wellbeing.

So I'm starting the conversation with some ideas of how we can more consciously create the world we wish to live in, but the expectation is never that we'll all be perfectly doing it all.

This is also not about switching off your office computer every night or recycling the paper you use, because we all know what we can do in those areas. These are ways of making a difference specifically as online businesses, not just to the planet, but to the individuals you reach with your content, the other creators you come into contact with, the services you use and so on.

(1) How We Run Our Businesses Day-to-Day

The pandemic and lockdown highlighted to the world that the way we have been working hasn't been serving us, and as business owners I want to see us own the fact that we are contributing to a huge shift in the way we earn a living. We get to prioritise our physical and mental health, the happiness of our families, the time we spend with our kids and the space we have to take care of ourselves. We get to model that to others and that is no small thing.

Of course, after a lifetime of conditioning around the importance of "hard work" and the daily reminders to hustle and push ourselves to the limits, there's unlearning required to get there. So many of us end up working harder, and for less pay, when we start working for ourselves. But let's not forget that we *can* choose to work less, we *can* design our businesses around our lives (rather than the other way around), we *can* choose not to conform to the way things have always been done, and doing so is in itself a radical act.

(2) Amplifying & Listening to a Diverse Range of Voices

"The moment that you have the idea to start your business, is the moment where inclusion should be a part of your strategy"

– Jayne Ashby, episode #86 of the *Quietly Ambitious* podcast

Most online business owners have a platform of some kind, and sometimes this involves inviting other business owners into certain projects. It's important that we consider which voices we get to amplify when we do so. For example, for my podcast interviews I have always gone out of my way to find new people, new voices and new opinions, and it makes for a *far* more interesting show that more people can relate to.

So many entrepreneurs are terrified of "getting it all wrong", but you must be willing to mess up along the way to doing the right thing.

I spoke to coach Jayne Ashby in Episode #86 of the *Quietly Ambitious* podcast about diversity and inclusion for small business owners and highly recommend listening to the full interview for more about what inclusivity means, why small business owners should be thinking about it, the fears that get in the way, and how we make this part of the conversation. My key takeaway, as Jayne so eloquently put it, was that "so much more growth happens when we get things wrong or when we fail"[29].

Even if you don't have the opportunity to feature others, this can apply to who you follow, the opinions you regularly listen to and the type of lives you see shared online. It's natural for us to end up in "bubbles" of people who look and think very similarly to us, but there's a whole world out there if you look.

(3) Making People Feel Seen, Heard & Welcome

Take radical responsibility for the experience of your right people at all stages of the journey with your business, from your free content to your most expensive offer. Do they feel valued? Do they feel seen? Do they feel safe? Do they feel heard? Are they able to access your content in its current format?

If you are building a platform online then you will mess up at some point, and you may be called out for something down the line. Be willing to get uncomfortable in the name of listening to the lived experience of your people. What can you learn? How can you show that

---

[29] You can listen to the full interview with Jayne Ashby in episode #86 of the *Quietly Ambitious* podcast here: https://ruthpoundwhite.com/episode-86-inclusivity-for-small-business-owners-with-jayne-ashby/

you're willing to do better, even if you don't yet know what doing better necessarily looks like?

It also doesn't take much effort to be more inclusive in our language (e.g. "they" instead of examples using he/she), to add your pronouns to your bio, or asking new clients if they have any access needs you should know about. It takes a little more effort to deliver your content in multiple formats (e.g. transcripts and closed captions for videos), but it's important to make the effort as you grow.[30] You can't do it all at once, but you can create an inclusivity and accessibility roadmap so that you stay committed to putting it all into place over time.

(4) The Accessibility of Your Offers

Accessibility isn't just about how you deliver content, it's about who can access it financially. As a sensitive entrepreneur, chances are you're already considering this, so here's what I most want you to know: not every single thing you offer has to be accessible to everyone, and you *must* prioritise financial sustainability in your own business first (or else you can't continue to help anybody).

As part of my regular inclusivity reviews, I considered the range of offers and content I have available to help business owners at different price points. I am confident in charging more for my courses and group programmes because I know that I also offer plenty of free and low-cost content alongside it.

---

[30] If you need more help with supporting your clients' access needs, listen to my interview with Kat Cuthbert on episode #87 of the Quietly Ambitious podcast here: https://ruthpoundwhite.com/episode-87-working-with-your-tendencies-unique-needs-as-a-human-with-kat-cuthbert/

You could also make a percentage of your work free, offering scholarship places once you've made enough sales, for example. Or offer pay-what-you-can places from time to time for your higher priced programmes (as long as doing so will not mean extra work for no pay for you). It is helpful to set clear boundaries around how and when you do this, as in my experience sensitive business owners can easily go too far the wrong way, leading to burnout, resentment and an unprofitable and unsustainable business.

(5) The Products & Services We Use

All online business owners make use of products, software and services to make our lives easier. It's worth asking yourself where you can support businesses run women and people from marginalised groups, and that are inclusive and values-led in their marketing. Sometimes there's no choice, or the difference in price is prohibitive, but I encourage you to invest your money wisely when you can.

(6) The Way We Work With Team Members

When we start growing a team as business owners, this puts us in a position of responsibility. We get to make sure all members of our team feel welcome, heard and valued. We might choose to hire those who are new and could use the support in getting their first testimonials (something Sara Tasker mentioned in episode #51 of the *Quietly Ambitious* podcast)[31], it could include training them, or giving them

---

[31] Listen to the full interview with Sara Tasker in episode #35 of the *Quietly Ambitious* podcast here: https://ruthpoundwhite.com/35-sara-tasker-on-money-influencer-responsibility-and-chronic-illness/

access to some of your services for free (I offer my team any of my courses, for example).

It also means being willing to pay for good work. Every time a team member raises their prices, I celebrate that. And to recognise that, as we are dismantling the traditional toxic ways of work for ourselves, this must also extend to our team members. Let's support them to live and work in a way that honours all of who they are, too.

(7) #OnlineActsofKindness & Supporting Other Creators

Early in my second business, I started a new hashtag on Instagram: #onlineactsofkindness. The idea behind it was to document the small things that we can do to support our online community. Instead of seeing everyone else as competition, celebrating and supporting one another benefits everyone.

The whole challenge and hashtag is about spotlighting others, sharing their work, giving them testimonials or telling them when you enjoy their content, stepping out of the shadows when we normally lurk, or by using their affiliate links when they recommend a product, and so on. If you can, show your appreciation by paying them. As Katie Sadler (@katiemorwenna), marketing consultant to authors, shared with me on Instagram: "giving someone who shares content for free that you love £3 a month via Patreon is a small but real way to say, 'I like what you do'."

(8) The Values We Embody

I shared above about how to uncover your core business values, but how much do you actually embody these values? Don't say one thing and do another. Take the time to regularly review how your values are playing out in your business to ask yourself where you can do better (and we can *always* do better, so don't beat yourself up if there's still room for improvement).

Don't stop there – share your values with your people. Kelly Diels has an incredible 'values and feminist practices' page on her website that she regularly references[32]. Add your values to your website, live them out, share them in your social media posts. The more we talk about our ideals, the more with (a) find we have in common with other people (b) connect with people who share the same values and (c) encourage others to consider how they are running their businesses or living their lives in alignment with their *own* values.

(9) The Way We Market & Sell

Yes, the way you sell what you do can make a difference. I wholeheartedly believe that it is possible to market your business in a compassionate, feminist, and intersectional way that does not put shame on any other people, does not put unnecessary pressure on people to buy, and keeps your values at the heart of everything.

Much of what I'm about to share was learned from feminist marketing consultant and coach for culture-makers, Kelly Diels. The way things have been traditionally done in the world of online marketing is to use certain psychological tactics that *work*. We're talking false scarcity, "pain points", promises of *the magic bullet,*

---

[32] See https://www.kellydiels.com/my-feminist-business-practices/

inflated income claims, or social "triggers"[33]. They encourage people to buy, but at what cost?

The good news is that we get to do things differently, so don't be afraid to sell! The research suggests that people do not need to be shamed or have their pain points triggered in order to buy. We get to start with common values and the desires of our clients instead. The more we market this way, the more we model it for others, and the less we all need to rely on triggers and manipulation.

(10) The Money You Make and the Wealth You Build

Finally, let's not forget **the world-changing benefits of wealth in the hands of a more diverse range of people.**

Making sure that you're getting paid and that you're meeting your income goals first will allow you to help more people in the long run. I could not offer pay-what-you-can spaces, for example, if I wasn't covering my time and energy in other ways. Earning more money also makes it easier to take time out to support other causes for free. For example, brand designer and creative mentor, Sarah Robertson (@thesearethedays.co) shared with me that she volunteers for charities and organisations that need her services – and she is able to do that thanks to all the paid work she does first.

You could take things even further and add a non-profit arm to your profit-making business. For example, you might run courses but then have a free academy that helps people from certain backgrounds or in certain positions to access what you do. You could also offer free training or heavily discounted products to charities etc.

---

[33]See https://www.kellydiels.com/fleb-marketing-tactic-9-social-triggers-social-conditions/

Making more money also makes it easier to support causes that matter to you. The Life You Can Save, founded by philosopher Peter Singer, is a fantastic resource for finding charities that use your money in the most cost-effective way. The idea behind it is that everyone should be donating a portion of their income. It can start as a tiny amount and grow as your profit grows. [34]

It's not all about donating money or time to causes that matter, though. Wealth brings power, and power in the hands of a more diverse range of humans is a very good thing. Wealth also brings far greater choice in what you spend money on, making it easier to support local and ethical businesses, or to give your family a better education than you had. If you're a human that cares about other humans, money will give you the power to act on that more freely.

(11) Eco-Friendly & Ethical Banking

The climate crisis ties into so many different social justice issues, and we all know about the usual advice to change our lightbulbs or recycle more, but how can business owners really make a difference in this area? One of the most powerful – but less obvious – answers is who you bank with.

Banks hold a lot of power in how they lend and invest our money. Consider switching your business and personal bank accounts to an ethical provider. You may have to do a little digging to discover their policies, though websites like ethicalconsumer.org are incredibly helpful in this area. Without doing this work, no matter how well-

---

[34] See thelifeyoucansave.org to learn more.

intentioned you are, your money will be supporting businesses that you don't believe in.

"Between them, 35 of the world's major banks... have provided $2.7 trillion (£2tn) to fossil fuel companies since the Paris Agreement on climate change was adopted at the end of 2015, according to a 2020 report from Rainforest Action Network and five other non-profits."

– From the BBC's *Smart Guide to Climate Change*[35]

(12) Your Unique Contribution

I want to encourage you to allow yourself to dream big in terms of the impact you want to have in your life and business. Some of your goals might not be possible yet, but that's the point! Allowing yourself to start talking about them – with your coach or with trusted friends – is the first step in making them happen. Whether they happen in the next few years, or the next few decades, can you get excited about the change you get to be a part of?

"You cannot get through a single day without having an impact on the world around you. What you do makes a difference, and you have to decide what kind of difference you want to make."

– Jane Goodall

And whatever you do, don't forget that playing to your strengths and following your bliss is a huge part of making a difference. Imagine if everyone did what mattered to them, if they worked in their unique zone of magic, how much happier would the world be? Don't be afraid to make a difference in your specific corner of the world, to charge what

---

[35] See https://www.bbc.com/future/article/20210126-how-you-invest-your-money-can-help-tackle-climate-change

you desire to charge to make it joyful and sustainable, and to believe that your work matters (because it really does).

CHAPTER 10: ARE YOU ALLOWING YOURSELF SUPPORT?

"If we want to change the world, we need change agents to know how to receive care."

– Emily & Amelia Nagoski, Burnout

Being quietly ambitious is about who you allow yourself to be and what you allow yourself to do. But it's also about being massively supported – and learning to ask for and accept that support in the first place. As simple as it may sound, the reality is that being supported was a huge journey for me – one that has been fundamental to my success as a business owner and how I feel in my life.

Three Reasons Why Being Supported Doesn't Always Come Naturally

It's not easy to ask for help. It's not easy to prioritise your feelings, your energy, your time, your joy. And there are very real reasons for it.

Reason Number 1: Conditioning

In their book, *Burnout*, Emily and Amelia Nagoski describe "Human Giver Syndrome" as the belief that you have a moral obligation to give everything of yourself to support other people. This is very common, but not exclusive to, women. After all, society associates womanhood and motherhood with caring and nurturing others, being highly attuned to the needs of others, taking care of the emotional and household labour in the family and juggling it all alongside looking great and going to work.

We all know women who just can't sit down. Maybe that woman is you. And is it any wonder when this is the message we have all grown up with? And doesn't it make sense that we might find it hard to even recognise where we need support – much less ask or pay for it – given that we are supposed to *be* the support?

This is what can make asking for support feel "selfish". It is difficult to admit that you want time to yourself, that you want to prioritise yourself, that you want some things to benefit you above everyone else. And, if you're an overachiever like me, it's difficult to let go of control, and the safety that "proving yourself" through doing it all can bring.

Although we absolutely don't need to justify it this way, it is helpful to remember that being supported doesn't just benefit you, it benefits everyone around you. You are setting an example to people who need permission to do the same (I have seen this time and time again when I share the ways in which I am supported with my clients, which we'll get to later on in this chapter) and you will simply be a better rested, more joyful human to be around.

"The deepest trauma women experience under patriarchy is that our lives, our bodies, and minds are not as valuable as men's. That we're worth less."

– Dr Valerie Rein, *Patriarchy Stress Disorder*

Whether you identify as a woman or not, all of this goes to highlight that something as simple as being supported can involve a lot of unlearning and deconditioning. Not to mention the discomfort that comes with being judged for claiming support (for example, women who hire cleaners, which we'll talk more about later), and with deeming yourself worthy of it in the first place.

Reason Number 2: Money & Worthiness

Not all support needs to be paid for, however money is a very real barrier for many of us. On the surface it might sound as simple as *"I can't afford the support I need right now"*, but there can be a lot going on under the surface of a statement like that.

Is it true that you can't afford it (in which case, fair enough), or is it that you won't prioritise spending money in that area?

Personally, I've found it fairly easy to invest in my business, to outsource specific tasks that were directly related to the money I made. But it has been far harder to invest in coaching to support me with how I feel, or money spent on personal care like a massage, a nice meal or even new clothes. A fixed amount of money spent on one thing can feel like an investment, and that same amount of money spent on something else can feel like an expense that you can't afford.

On first thought that might appear to make complete sense – of course investing in support to make money is worth it, and the latter feels riskier because you're not quite sure what the "return on investment" might be, or whether it'll even end up being the right thing (we've all spent money on things we ultimately didn't enjoy). But isn't all support valid and "worth it" if it improves your life in some way?

The truth is that there doesn't need to be a return on investment beyond how you feel. We are all worthy and deserving of giving ourselves more headspace, of feeling more pleasure and of experiencing more joy. The likelihood is that it *will* have a positive ripple effect: in the time you're able to spend with your family, in the quality of your work when you get to stay in your "zone of magic", perhaps even in your productivity. But you are worth spending money on regardless.

Reason Number 3: Vulnerability

You know by now that I'm a huge introvert, and part of what that looks like for me is being incredibly private. In order to start claiming the support I needed, I had to overcome the hurdle of opening up to other people in the first place. Claiming support is a brave and vulnerable act.

As business owners, one of the most important ways we can be supported is to have someone to guide us through the feelings. I'm sure you'll resonate with the idea that being in business is the best form of self-development there is (and it's not always what we thought we were originally signing up for).

Feelings creep in at every stage of the journey. *What does it mean about us when our posts aren't getting the engagement they used to? Do people not like me if they aren't buying my stuff? Am I a failure if I had a launch flop?* They can lead to spinning your wheels, procrastinating, trying to prove yourself, distracting yourself and getting in the way of what you *really* want to be doing.

Having a coach or community or mastermind group to help us through all of this *is* a luxury. And it's also something I see as non-negotiable in my business. Receiving coaching, as well as being supported by peers, has changed everything for me – not just in my business, but across all areas of my life. And it all required me to be vulnerable and to be seen in a way I never had been before.

Whenever somebody new signs up to work with me 1:1 – and especially in my group coaching programme, where it's a little easier to hide or to compare yourself to others – I will always let them know that it's not enough simply to be there. Learning to take up space to *claim* the support they need is as much a part of the journey as anything else, and it takes an active commitment to do so, especially when it feels uncomfortable to ask a "silly question", to share how you're really feeling, or when all you really want to do is close yourself off from other people.

Being supported in this way in your business is really quite magical. Making decisions and running a business more or less on your own is hard. We all have strengths and weaknesses. We all have doubts. And we all have an invisible glass ceiling of what we feel is possible for us (see Chapter 13). When we are vulnerable to others, they get to reflect our true greatness back to us.

Six Areas Where Being Supported Has Transformed My Life

Before we dive into how you can be more supported as a quietly ambitious business owner, let's talk about comparison. It's so easy to compare what we're doing (or not doing) to other people. I have a young child and I have a successful business under my belt that I quit to run a second successful business. I also create a lot and, at this stage, have several workshops and programs out there, at the same time as being a sensitive, introverted and chronically tired human.

It's natural to compare your own output and to ask why it isn't so easy for you to do all of the same. But the problem with comparing yourself to random people on the internet is that you have no idea what they're really dealing with, and what support systems they have in place. And in this chapter I'll share some of mine with you.

(1) Advice, Inspiration & Community

Advice, inspiration and a likeminded community of people could be found in the form of podcasts, social media accounts, Facebook groups, blogs, email newsletters and so on. In the earlier days of my business this is where I found most of my support, and it was free! Although I could have greatly benefitted from investing in the right coach earlier on, I am so grateful for the spaces I found freely available.

The flip side is that things can feel "noisy" when you're listening to anyone and everyone. It's overwhelming when someone over here says you have to do things this way, and someone over there seems to completely contradict it all. This is where discernment comes in: who do you listen to?

When I started my first business in 2008, the landscape was a little different. Running an online business in the way I was doing it was still fairly new, and I latched onto anyone I found talking about it (without really considering whether they were the *right* people). I listened to the loudest voices, but I didn't consider myself to fit in with them and was disconnected from what I thought I had to do to market myself online.

Thank goodness for the fact that there are so many wonderful humans to learn from. As much as we are the right person for our right people in our own business, we also have our "right people" to learn from. Whether you prefer a kick-you-up-the-arse motivational style, or a softer and more intuitive approach, you get to find the people that resonate with you.

There's no one, magic, "right" way to do this. You get to follow those that make you feel seen and understood, and leave the rest behind.

(2) Coaching & Mentoring

Free support can be wonderful, especially when you're just getting started, but when you can afford it, I highly recommend finding a coach, mentor, or a mastermind group. There's huge transformation to be had in these intimate environments, especially when you have "skin in the game", financially.

It can feel scary, risky and uncomfortable to invest in your business, but sometimes that stretch is *exactly* what gets you to a place of deciding that you're making it happen, no matter what. Only you can decide what's a stretch you can afford to make vs. a genuine case of affordability. If you're in the position to make it work somehow, there is tremendous power in this kind of support.

I don't think we should underestimate the power of having space to talk about your feelings as they relate to your business. Having that space, having that time in calls or meetings dedicated to you on a regular basis, having someone you can email or message when you're having a wobble, all that means so much. No matter what advice they ultimately give you, having that space *in itself* can make a big difference.

Which is why it's so important to choose somebody you resonate with. Someone who sees you, won't judge you, but is willing to stretch you in the name of who you are and what you want. I have been supported by coaches – both 1:1 and in several groups – continuously since before I even started this business in 2018 and, as I said above, this kind of support is now non-negotiable for me.

My coaches have inspired me to show up wholeheartedly as myself, they've made it clear when I needed to raise my prices despite my huge doubts, they've helped me to move past feelings of impostor syndrome, or fears of what might happen if I succeed. In short, they've massively expanded what's possible for me in my life and business.

Paying for this support was and always is uncomfortable for me. But it has always been worth it in so many ways (not just financial).

(3) Spiritual & Healing Practices

There's an important difference between coaching and therapy and, in my experience, both are important ways to be supported in your life and business.

More recently I have invested in several complementary therapies and spiritual practices. Meditation, breathwork, spiritual retreats, intuitive movement sessions... all of it fills my cup and supports my nervous system in different ways.

(4) My Own Self-Support Toolkit

Aside from the free and paid-for support already mentioned, I have my own toolkit that I use on a regular basis. And the biggest thing that has supported me in creating this toolkit – and knowing when to call upon it – is self-awareness.

As you know, for me, journalling is a real, solid form of support that has also made me more aware of what I need on any given day. It's like self-coaching, meditation, brainstorming, and idea generation all rolled into one. It's brilliant, and it's something that I can do absolutely on my own.

Other tools in my arsenal include connecting with myself through meditation, singing, dancing, getting out in nature, running, gardening plus fancy meals out, luxury hotels, childcare and regular mini-breaks! All of this counts as support, and they all help me to create headspace and increase the capacity I have for joy.

(5) Practical Business Support

As I mentioned earlier, when I started investing in support, spending money on the practical stuff felt a lot easier than anything else. That said, time and time again I see clients struggling to do it all, afraid to commit to this kind of spending in their business.

Know that you can start off *very* small when outsourcing in your business. I started with ad-hoc projects and a virtual assistant (VA) on a very small number of hours per month, and I increased as and when I could. My VA now supports me with anything from creating graphics to social media to setting up funnels for my evergreen courses and workshops.

As my friend, mastermind sister and Certified Online Business Manager Willemijn Maas shared with me on episode #84 of the Quietly Ambitious podcast, it is crucial that we set up systems in our businesses that mean it can keep running even if we can't physically or mentally work on it.[36]

(6) Domestic Support

Finally, allow me to get on my soapbox for a little while. I couldn't do what I do without massive support with childcare and management of the home. This kind of support is so often overlooked in our society because it is traditionally "women's work", but it is crucial to the survival and growth of my business (as well as my own sanity as a human).

Millionaire business owner Denise Duffield-Thomas, author of *Chillpreneur,* put it brilliantly and opened up an incredible discussion

---

[36] Listen to the full interview with Willemijn Mass on episode #84 of the *Quietly Ambitious* podcast here: https://ruthpoundwhite.com/episode-84-systems-support-in-business-at-any-stage-with-willemijn-maas/

around this topic in her article titled 'I'm a self-made millionaire, and this is EXACTLY how much help I have at home',[37] and this is how it begins:

"A man would never need to write this article because it's just assumed that they have a wife at home doing most of the housework and childcare.

But for some reason, a woman outsourcing home help is secretive and taboo. I'm afraid of being told I'm lazy, out of touch or a bad mother, despite the fact that my husband benefits too!

I feel like I have to defend and add disclaimers to almost every paragraph. Yes, I know I'm lucky. Yes, I know nobody is really "self-made" (white privilege hello!), yes I know there are single mothers and struggling families who can't afford help.

Lots of people ask me how I balance it all (ah, the age-old question for successful women) and the honest answer is WITH SO MUCH PAID HELP."

- Denise Duffield-Thomas

So let's not judge ourselves or others for hiring a cleaner, for not cooking healthy meals from scratch each night, or for paying for support with childcare. As Denise says: "housework is practically the only job in the world that's supposed to be fulfilling for women to do for free (how convenient) but somehow shameful and exploitative to pay another woman (and it's mostly women) to do it". The guilt is not

---

[37] See https://medium.com/@deniseduffieldthomas/im-a-self-made-millionaire-and-this-is-exactly-how-much-help-i-have-at-home-c15c46d9feee

serving any of us. We cannot do it all alone in our businesses, and that is also true for our lives and homes.

To conclude this chapter, I want to invite you to consider where you could be more supported in your life and business. It could be something as simple as ordering healthy meals so that you don't need to cook once a week. It could be asking your partner to permanently take over the laundry. It could mean investing in a coach, mastermind group or regular massages. It could mean reducing the number of people you follow to those that truly inspire you and add value to your day. It could be hiring someone to mow your lawn!

And it all starts with deciding that you are worthy of investing in. Not just in the areas where a return on investment is more likely, but in ways that bring you joy and free up mental space.

You are worthy of having the support that you need to grow your business. You are worthy of having the support that you desire to live the live you want to live.

CHAPTER 11: HONOURING OUR NATURAL CYCLES OF CREATION (& PRIORITISING REST)

A huge part of honouring who I am as a quietly ambitious business owner has been to recognise my internal seasons. Knowing when to rest and when to get visible. Understanding that it's ok that I don't always feel like I have something that I want to share.

Building a business is about so much more than what we achieve and the money that we make. It is *totally* possible to run a business that is both profitable and incredibly fulfilling *and* that honours our natural energy levels.

To do so, we have to think carefully about our beliefs around what it means to be "productive", and learn to trust ourselves to listen to our own inner seasons.

How I Recovered from Entrepreneurial Burnout (Or... Why I Gave up the Hustle)

Unfortunately, so many entrepreneurs have their own burnout story. When I first started working online, it was all about "the hustle", getting as much done as possible, and working hard now so that you can live your life later. Thankfully the conversation has moved on since then, but that doesn't necessarily mean that we don't feel pressure to force ourselves to work until we hit burnout. Maybe we feel we have something to prove, or maybe it's simply that the societal conditioning runs *strong*.

You already know a lot of my story: how I started almost by accident, how I wasn't sure who to follow that aligned with my way of marketing, and how I massively undervalued my services and undercharged accordingly. All of that was a recipe for burnout.

Writing as much as I could at rock-bottom rates quickly took all of the joy out of my craft. I felt like a machine, and the impact of that lasted for many years. I learned my lesson, charged more money and hired other writers so that I could work less. I was doing better, but I filled that free time I created with, you guessed it, more work!

It might surprise you to learn that, as much as I preach rest and doing less, I am a natural overachiever and workaholic. As I mentioned in the chapter on being visible and scared, doing more can be a manifestation of self-doubt, and that was certainly true for me.

I wasn't happy. My husband wasn't happy with me. Physically I could just about handle it, but mentally I was stressed, anxious, unfulfilled and fed up with life – the opposite of the "entrepreneurial dream". I ended up taking drastic action and convincing my husband to come travelling for a year in Southeast Asia. I still worked while we were away, but it was on a much more relaxed schedule and I started to think differently about my work.

My eyes started to be opened to the belief that I had to work very hard to make good money. I realised that I didn't need to work nine-to-five, Monday to Friday. I took time out in the middle of the day, and I stopped feeling guilty about it. I sometimes worked on weekends.

When I trained for a marathon, I reduced my work hours dramatically to account for long runs and recovery. I embraced the slower pace in my work, focused on doing less, and decided that making it work was not contingent on "doing it all". I can see clearly when I look back over the journey of my business that when I focused on only *one* way of doing things, my business grew so much more quickly.

Doing It All With Limited Capacity (& Redefining Productivity)

Having a child added a whole new dimension to these learnings. No longer could I work all hours – I needed childcare for focused work time, and I had no option to prioritise rest during the day when my sleep was broken for the first 18 months of his life (and beyond, just less consistently!) I was growing a new coaching business while running my old copywriting one. I was no longer just responsible for myself.

And then, when my son was two, the pandemic and lockdown happened. No more childcare, from nursery or from family, and we were all suddenly thrown into the anxiety of facing this new, previously unimaginable reality.

Just after lockdown started I began to experience life-altering fatigue. When I say life-altering fatigue I mean: days spent in bed (often), flu-like body pains, a massive change in my day-to-day activities, taking days to recover from exerting myself, radical prioritisation (and re-prioritisation), brain fog that hugely affects my productivity, accepting I can't do a lot of what I want to and then fighting against that. And all the mental stuff that comes with that.

I have good periods and bad periods. Two years later I still don't have an official diagnosis, and from the outside you wouldn't be able to tell there was anything wrong with me, but it has massively affected the way that I need to live and work.

Before I experienced these symptoms, I knew that our work culture was toxic. I knew that our worth as humans should not be tied to productivity. I knew that we needed to find a way to build our businesses around our personality and energy levels.

And it only made me more fired up about building a business that allows us to rest and take care of ourselves. Not in a bubble-bath kind of way but in a deep, real and even selfish way. A lot of the time I have no choice but to pause and slow down, and as difficult as that is there are so many valuable lessons in what I have experienced.

I create a lot in my business, and if you're wondering "how I do it all" then I'll share more of the truth behind the output in the next chapter. But what I want to share here is that I have now totally redefined my relationship to productivity.

I waste a lot of time. Sometimes the brain fog makes it feel like a simple task can take hours, and sometimes I just flit around from one thing to the next. But what I've learned is that once I am able to follow my flow, what happens even in the space of one hour can be magical (and the rest of it is just part of my process).

As difficult as it can be to let go of old, corporate ways of working, we get to do things differently as business owners. This isn't about clocking in and out at set times of the day. It's about learning what lights us up, how we can access the highest part of ourselves that *knows* what to do, how we can fuel our creativity. That's the new definition of productivity that I can stand behind.

Everybody has the right to work in a way that supports their physical & mental wellbeing, and that leaves time to enjoy actually living. It may take some figuring out - plus a LOT of unlearning - but we can change the way things are done.

Working With Our Natural Cycles

The new definition of productivity must also take into account our natural cycles.

Modern society generally views time and life as linear: we are born, we grow, we reach different milestones through childhood, adolescence and adulthood, and our bodies age with the passing of time. The way we measure our time through calendars - and how much time we have available to make things happen in our lives - is manmade, and for *so* many of us (especially sensitive business owners), it creates a pressure and a constant need to keep "doing".

But nature is cyclical: the earth, moon and sun all move in repeating elliptical patterns. And, as a result, we experience a cycle of seasons and moon phases (even our phases of sleep) that govern so much of how we feel, what we focus on and how we live our lives. Our ancestors relied on these cyclical signs and rhythms to live their lives and go about their daily activities.

Most of us now have to live our lives by the calendar and the 24-hour clock for practical reasons, but we can still benefit from tuning into cycles and seasons.

We all have a general feeling of what the different seasons mean for the energy of our creativity, visibility, culmination and rest in our body and in our business.

- Winter is the "fertile void" where, on the surface, it may not appear as though much is happening, but a lot of work is going on unseen (and it is the hardest season to embrace, which is why we'll talk more about that in detail later).
- Eventually that activity becomes evident in spring, where nature quite rapidly "springs" into action.
- The green shoots appear, the flowers start to bloom, and it all reaches a climax throughout the summer, when the days are long and we all have much more productive time to enjoy.
- Things – literally and metaphorically – culminate and are ready to be harvested come autumn, before dying back again for winter.

The four seasons of nature have been naturally linked to two other cycles that can have a powerful impact in our lives: the menstrual cycle and the lunar cycle. And they each have so much to teach us about working in harmony with all that we are.

Important Note: Everyone is Different

We are all different, and while many will identify with the patterns of energy experienced through the seasons, moon phases and stages of the menstrual cycle, others will not. It's also completely normal for some cycles to feel more "typical" than others.

So don't worry if your feelings don't correspond with what's shared here. The most important thing is that you get in the habit of tuning into your own energy, learning from that and working in a way that honours you as an individual going forward. And, for those who do not menstruate, know that most of the lessons will still be relevant to you. As always: feel free to skip what doesn't serve you.

How to Work With Each of the Cycles

Disclaimer: before I describe each of the seasons, please know I'm no medical or moon expert! Use these as a guide for your own exploration. And remember, not everyone identifies with the feelings and energies listed below, and that's ok.

(1) Winter/ New Moon/ Menstrual Phase

The inner winter phase lasts from day 1 of the cycle (the start of the bleed) for up to 7 days, where it is normal to feel tired and energetically that you're "letting go". In terms of the lunar cycle, it includes the days leading up to, during and just after the new moon (when there is no visible moon in the sky). When it comes to manifestation, the new moon is seen as the most powerful time to set intentions on what you want to manifest over the coming cycle.

This winter phase is all about inner focus and reflection. Whether you're an introvert or not, you'll usually feel most introverted during your inner winter. It can be a good opportunity to spend some time alone to reflect on the past cycle, or simply to rest. Above all else, listen to what your body is telling you, and do your best to honour that (and always being kind to yourself if everyday life doesn't allow for it!)

(2) Spring/ Waxing Moon/ Follicular Phase

The waxing moon is a phase of growth towards the full moon - the days either side of the first quarter moon. It corresponds with nature's spring, where energy is visibly speeding up and things are growing - and the follicular phase of the menstrual cycle, which is when eggs start to mature in the ovaries in preparation for ovulation.

The inner spring phase is all about starting to feel more energised and motivated again, perhaps letting new ideas emerge that you might feel ready to take action on. It's a time where we naturally feel more creative and might start making plans, but it's also important to keep tuning into what your body needs as you become more active.

(3) Summer/ Full Moon/ Ovulation Phase

Next, we have summer. Everything is at its peak! Including the menstrual cycle, where an egg is released and energy levels are usually at their highest (if you have a 28-day cycle, ovulation happens around day 14). This is linked to the full moon phase of the lunar cycle, where the moon is big and bright, and many of us will feel more energised and less able to sleep soundly. When it comes to manifestation, the full moon is seen as a powerful time to let go of what no longer serves you (some may burn a list of things under the light of the moon), in order to continue to manifest your intentions from the new moon.

Inner summer is a time to be visible, to be seen, to socialise, to invite people into what you do. Whether you're an extrovert or not, summer will usually be when you feel your most outgoing. Summer is a great time to be seen and heard, as we are often at our most confident. But be wary of making too many plans while you're full of energy - try to pace yourself in anticipation of the upcoming autumn/ fall.

(4) Autumn/ Waning Moon/ Luteal Phase

The autumn/fall of the menstrual cycle begins just after ovulation. The egg is either fertilised or the womb gets ready to shed its lining. With the shift in hormones may come cravings for comfort food, a desire to slow down, a drop in energy levels and symptoms of PMS (including mood swings). In the lunar cycle, this is the waning moon - the days either side of the third quarter moon, as we head back towards another new moon.

The inner autumn can sometimes be challenging for people, but the more you lean into it and track it, the more you can utilise its power. It's a great time for tying up loose ends and checking tasks off your to do lists that you missed in your summer energy. As a business owner, you may not feel like being so visible during this phase, and your mind may start to make you doubt your work. Trust is hugely importance during our inner autumn: trust your past self for the plans they put in place, and trust your future self for their ability to execute them well.

Rest Is Part of the Work

One of the hardest things about working with these seasons is honouring our need to rest. In a culture that prioritises output and productivity – and especially for those of us who identify as "overachievers" – doing nothing can be the hardest phase of all.

The winter season is often characterised by a lack of ideas or a lack of motivation. Try as you might, it's hard to access that state of flow when you push yourself to keep doing. And it's scary: what if you stop making money? What if you never come up with the next right thing to put out into the world? What if people forget about you and your business?

The reason this season is called the "fertile void" is because, as in nature, the pause comes before the next shoots appear. As Kate Northrup, author of *Do Less: A Revolutionary Approach to Time and Energy Management for Ambitious Women, describes it:* "Deep, true creativity doesn't emerge despite the deep pause. It emerges because of it."[38]

How To Prioritise Rest

As a business owner, you'll relate to the fact that your to-do list never ends. The key is knowing that it's okay that you'll never get through that to-do list. You have to build the evidence to trust that taking time to rest lays the groundwork for everything else to fall into place.

Practically speaking it means being willing to radically prioritise and let things go. Even the most ambitious humans can't achieve it all at once (especially when they're not well-rested). The book *Drop the Ball: Achieving More by Doing Less* by Tiffany Dufu gave me new guiding questions to support me in my inner winter: *"what can I drop the ball on? How can I make this easier?"*.

The truth is that letting go of things that some parts of you want to do is uncomfortable. Choosing not to be productive is uncomfortable. Taking a nap in the middle of the day while somebody else is caring for your child, or your clients are asking you questions, or there are bills that need to be paid is all uncomfortable.

And rest is also boring! It's not all spa days, luxury hotels and having healthy meals cooked for you. It is time spent lying in bed, binge-watching TV shows, it's not answering your emails for a week, it's awkwardly asking your partner to help you do something you

---

[38] Read Kate Northrup's full blog post on the "fertile void" here: https://katenorthrup.com/four-phases-creation-part-three-fertile-void/

should be doing yourself, or letting your garden grow wild because taking care of it is not currently a priority.

It's also making decisions in your business, even when you're feeling full of energy and ideas, that allow space and time for rest. It's taking on fewer clients at higher prices, not making yourself available for meetings on certain days of the week, sometimes cancelling client calls or saying no to projects that you wouldn't mind being part of. It can look like choosing the *one* thing that will move the needle in your business and forgetting everything else.

All of this can be uncomfortable to do, but over time you build up the evidence that *resting really works*. Not only do you start to feel better, but you discover that your ability to make money is actually supported by your need to rest.

Rest is Also About Self-Trust

If you're going to learn to rest when you need to, then you need to learn to listen to both your mind and your body. In my work, "rest" isn't just about doing less (or nothing at all), it's also an acronym that stands for:

Radical

Entrepreneurial

Self

Trust

We need to learn to trust our body's need to rest, and we need to trust in ourselves as business owners if we're going to have the courage to build a business that supports all of our needs.

- We need to trust ourselves in the moments where the noise on the internet is telling us something different to the thing that's in our heart.

- We need to trust ourselves when we have a "nudge" to create something new, even though our brain is trying to protect us by giving us all of the reasons why this just won't work.

- We need to trust ourselves to take time out, to step back, to do things differently in a culture that ties our self-worth to productivity and a very limited number of markers for success.

- We need to trust ourselves to be the leaders we were meant to be, especially as sensitive humans who have been raised in a culture with very limited examples of what leadership "should" look like for people like us.

- We need to trust ourselves to break free from - and play a part in changing - the norms of marketing, business, work, and whatever other unhelpful (maybe even toxic) beliefs come up in your particular industry.

We cannot cultivate this trust in ourselves if we never take time to pause and go inwards.

Trust in yourself is *not* the same as complete confidence. Trust is more akin to self-compassion and building your ability to deal with whatever happens vs. building confidence based on what does or does not happen. Your self-trust is something that you get to practice completely independently of external results (although if you keep going, you *will* see the results to help you build it more quickly - and you *will* still fail in future, too).

Here's how Kristin Neff describes the benefits of self-compassion vs self-esteem in her book (with my notes in square brackets) *Self Compassion* (which I highly recommend by the way).

"When our sense of self-worth stems from being a human being intrinsically worthy of respect [by practicing self-compassion]—rather than being contingent on obtaining certain ideals [by building self-esteem]—our sense of self-worth is much less easily shaken."

In short, self-trust is a way of being, a willingness to step back from the here and now and to commit to yourself and an unknown future. Confidence is a feeling that may come and go, but your ability to practice self-trust is always there (even if it's sometimes harder to find).

So how do you learn to trust in yourself? It all begins in the winter/rest phase of the cycle. Connecting to and listening to what your intuition is trying to tell you. Always developing that awareness of your thoughts. Identifying and connecting with the thing that makes what you do completely unique. And then simply deciding that you – in all your imperfect glory – are already a leader, and you get to make choices and take aligned action in your business based on deciding that.

CHAPTER 12: HOW I DO IT ALL (& THE POWER OF IMPERFECT EXPERIMENTATION)

We've talked about why rest is so important, and how it's completely normal to experience "fallow" phases in our lives and businesses. But how does this look, practically speaking, when you have a business to run, money to make, and products to sell?

When I reflect on the four years since I started my second business, I have created a *lot*. And I am regularly asked how I do it all, alongside being a huge advocate for doing less, following what feels good and, of course, resting!

So here's how I do it, in a way that honours my body.

My Four Key Creation Strategies

As you know, I started this business after a decade running a copywriting company. Where the first business took me *years* to reach a decent level of income, I was able to achieve it in a fraction of the time in my second business – while dealing with sleepless nights, lockdowns and fatigue. I put this down to four key strategies.

Strategy 1: Imperfect Experimentation

When I started my second business, I gave myself complete permission to figure things out as I went. It was the mindset of "imperfect experimentation".

On the surface it's easy: just put things out there, see what feels good and what works, and learn your lessons before doing it again (or moving onto the next thing). The reality isn't quite that simple. It requires radical self-trust in the face of the unknown. You're trying new things to see what happens, and that usually requires stretching your comfort zone.

What makes it easier is deciding that you'll learn from the results, no matter what they may be. Which has led to brilliant momentum in a very short space of time. Once I had that momentum, I was able to leverage it in other ways: investing money into support, inviting people from different programmes to work with me more closely, and being able to quickly test, tweak and improve my way of doing things.

Don't get me wrong – it wasn't as neat and tidy as it may sound. The way it played out was messy: I started putting content out there and building my audience before I even knew what I was selling, I have had many failed launches where nobody signed up, and I flitted around different topics based on whatever I felt like creating at the time. Which brings me to my next strategy.

Strategy 2: I Followed What Felt Good

Most business advice focuses on a clear strategy: decide on a signature offer, set up all of your content to funnel people to that offer. Make sure everything you do serves that signature offer. Stick to one topic and don't confuse your audience by doing too much.

This advice is not *wrong*, but it can put a lot of pressure on us to (a) know exactly what we want to do from the beginning (most of us don't) and (b) force ourselves to work only on that even when we have other ideas.

Because I gave myself permission to experiment, I was able to make decisions based on whatever felt good at the time. As we've explored throughout this book, I spend a lot of time getting to know and understand myself. One thing I know to be true is that anything that feels fun or gives me "the tingles" is a lot less work than something I think I "should" be doing.

Knowing that I'm excited about creating a programme collapses the time it takes for me to create it. Which is one big way in which I get more done.

Sometimes that looks like going through a phase of creating new and different offers in succession. Sometimes it looks like effortlessly "downloading" a new programme (like my Quiet Ambition course[39]) and re-launching it several times within the space of a few months. I choose what feels good to me at the time.

It has been four years and I have several courses and programmes out there at this point, but it's all cumulative. They are all based on my over-arching philosophy, but they vary in topic and delivery. Early on it didn't necessarily appear to "make sense", but by this stage I am so grateful that I allowed myself to experiment, follow the feelings and build up my body of work in this way.

Strategy 3: Redefining Consistency

You must put yourself out there consistently to build momentum in your business. But showing up consistently, for me, is absolutely not about doing things on a set, rigid schedule – and I rarely have all of my content and offers planned out far in advance (see strategy 2 above).

---

[39] See https://ruthpoundwhite.com/quiet-ambition/

Forcing myself to show up every day is simply not going to work for me as a sensitive introvert. In fact, I doubt that most humans – with their natural energy ebbs and flows – are able to hold themselves to a rigid schedule when they don't yet have a team behind them. So how can we achieve what feels unachievable?

To take my business as an example, I set the intention that I am *always* showing up, even when I take time away. One day you'll see a new podcast episode from me, or an email come into your inbox (which may have been written that day, or may be repurposed from months or years ago). The next day you'll see me on Instagram stories or sharing a post on my profile. And then I might disappear from public view for a couple of days.

I have no fixed posting schedule. I try to send newsletters once a week, but beyond that I follow my energy. What never changes, though, is my *intention:* **I am *always* showing up and building momentum in my business, even when I take time away.** And the more I create, the more I get to repurpose, the easier it is to be outwardly visible without actually needing to "be there" all the time.

Consistency is about the momentum of putting your work out into the world over time. Sometimes that looks like visibly showing your face on Instagram Stories. Sometimes that looks like sending emails, or posting once a week. Sometimes it looks like a pause, or doing the bigger picture work behind the scenes. But it never looks like a complete shutdown, and the momentum is always pulling things forward.

Strategy 4: Repurpose & Let It Be Easy

You may not realise it, but this book is the most magnificent example of repurposing my content. Almost everything you're reading here has been created by me already, it has just never been put together in quite this way. And that is another reason why I am able to create so much.

I keep track of and re-use old newsletters on a regular basis, I use the exact same content when I re-launch something I've already launched in the past, I make sure to sell the same offers again and again, and some of my podcast episodes started out as blog posts. I also have a note in my phone full of content drafts from the phases in my cycle when I feel most chatty and inspired.

It's totally fine to be visible for a while and then to retreat and hide away. Sometimes you might notice that I don't show up for a while, but more often than not you'll still receive my emails, see new podcast episodes being published or have the opportunity to join courses that I've run in the past because I'm not afraid to make things easier for myself by repurposing, re-using and re-launching.

Don't Compare Your Journey to Mine

Before we end this chapter, I need to be completely honest with you: I am not perfect. There are times when I absolutely do push myself too hard, my fatigue flares up and I beat myself up about it (though I'm far more likely to show myself compassion these days). There are times where I force myself to create something because the "shoulds" got a little too loud. There are times when I resist creating the thing that feels really good because something about it scares me.

I teach what I need to learn. I am a work-in-progress and every time I share this message in my content and with my clients, every time I ask someone where they are in their cycle, every time I ask you where you can drop the ball, I am reminding myself to trust what my body and intuition are trying to tell me.

This is why I am deeply supported, and why support is non-negotiable for me. Just ask my mastermind sisters about my relationship with rest (or listen to episode #97 of the podcast, where we all discuss what rest means to us)[40].

And don't forget that it's easy to look at somebody else's output and think that they have it all together, that they have greater capacity than you or more time to work than you do. Don't underestimate the importance of time in building your body of work, and remember that your journey is your journey for a reason. It's not a competition.

It's true that I have created an incredible body of work over the last four years, but it took me a decade of figuring out who I was before I was ready to start putting my face out there and experimenting.

Believe it or not, I procrastinated for around three years when I first had the idea to start this new business. And when I did, I had the incredible benefit of still earning money in my old business to invest in my new one from the beginning. Including huge amounts of coaching and practical support that greatly increased the speed at which I was able to make things happen. Not to mention learning to listen to myself to collapse the time it takes to come up with and follow through on a new idea.

Your journey is your journey for a reason. Whatever you're seeing somebody else creating, you never know the full picture of what it took

---

[40] See https://ruthpoundwhite.com/97-rest-trusting-your-body-a-conversation-with-my-mastermind-group/

to get there. And your own journey will *always* feel slower than the highlight reel you see of other people.

As much as we want it all to happen at once, every single step you're taking now is adding up to create the body of work that only you can create. Just be willing to experiment, follow your feelings and set the intention that you're *always* showing up.

CHAPTER 13: IDENTIFYING YOUR UNIQUE GLASS CEILING OF POSSIBILITY

You've probably heard of the glass ceiling theory, which references the invisible upper limit on the careers of women and minority groups based on external discrimination.

To own and unapologetically go for what you in your life and business, it's important to look at what your own glass ceiling is. As entrepreneurs we may not be working in the traditional corporate roles that the original glass ceiling theory was most commonly applied to, so we get to explore this idea slightly differently.

What I mean by the *glass ceiling* is that we have all grown up with layers of identities – labels, lived experiences and ideas about the "type of person" we are – that add up to create an invisible limit to what we think is possible or what we think we're allowed to want and ask for. I call these limits that can go with a label or an identity *stories*.

For example, as a sensitive person, my story was that my feelings were too much and so I learned to hide them away. As an introvert, the story was that I was not "the right kind of person" to market myself and put myself out there online. As a woman, the story was that my ambition was a negative quality, and this was especially true after I became a mother, very aware that I didn't fit the traditional "maternal" or "nurturing" boxes. I also have stories about being the breadwinner, about relationships, and about any identity I've been associated with.

All the labels, identities, and roles that we play or have played in our life come together to create this unique glass ceiling of what you believe you're allowed to do and what you think is possible. They create an invisible "rulebook" of how we live, what we achieve, what we want, and who we be.

Your own glass ceiling is going to look different to mine. Maybe you didn't have access to a good education, or have parents who helped you to aim high when you were growing up, so you created a story around the limits of what you could achieve. You might be a person of colour; you might be feeling the effects of generations of systemic oppression. Maybe you took on the identity of "the good mother" from your own mother, maybe you have always felt like an outcast, or maybe you've always rebelled against authority. Whatever your unique set of identities may be, they all come together to create your individual glass ceiling.

These are identities – and stories about what they mean – that you have been collecting ever since you were a child, which is why you can't see the ceiling (although you may know that something is limiting you). Which is why the first step is, always, awareness. You have to see it before you can break through it, before you can ask yourself how things might get to be different.

***

Exercise: Exploring Your Identities

There are many ways to start bringing these identities and stories to light. Here's an exercise taken from my Quiet Ambition course as an example[41]:

(1) List out words that people may have used to describe you as a child (e.g. shy, bossy, hyperactive, naughty), words based on your personality (empathetic, sensitive, introverted), identities based around your views and beliefs (feminist, vegetarian, religious, spiritual), or anything else that comes to mind (e.g. physical appearance and abilities, experiences you've gone through, cultural background, habits etc.)

(2) It's also relevant to think about the roles you play in life now (e.g. wife, mother, daughter, friend) and how people (including yourself!) might describe or perceive you in those roles (e.g. the brainy sibling, the devoted mother, the reliable friend)

(3) Next, go through this list and pick some of the top labels that stand out the most. You might instantly know why a particular label is important to work on now, or it could be a feeling in your body that you can't quite explain that tells you to dig a little deeper. Whatever it is, pick a few to work on now.

(4) Now dig into some of these roles and labels using some journaling prompts (by the way, it's totally ok if you don't have all the answers. You're starting the uncovering, it's not a quick fix):
- *What story have you created around what's possible based on this label?*

---

[41] You can find out more about the Quiet Ambition course here: https://ruthpoundwhite.com/quiet-ambition/

- How does labelling yourself in this way affect your day-to-day choices, actions, your schedule, the way you work in your business?
- How does labelling yourself in this way affect what you offer, your prices, your services or products?
- What does this label mean for you in terms of how others will see you, in your life & business?

(5) Now be honest with yourself. Which of those labels are serving you? Which do you want to remove? Which labels do you want to take on instead, if any?

This is not something that will always be easy to do on your own, nor is it something that'll always lead to immediate answers. But even scratching the surface of the layers of who you are and who you think you should be can open you up to new, incredible ideas of what's possible.

***

There may be some identities that you are immediately ready to let go of, but for most of us it's not that simple. Conscious awareness is helpful, but in the moment – when you're making plans, setting goals, pricing your offers, deciding what's possible – your unconscious beliefs will kick into gear.

Your glass ceiling is why your brain will say things like, *I want X, but I can't do that because of Y* – and why it'll sound very logical and believable and will play out in your decisions. For example, you might want to take a 3 month trip abroad and come up with a list of logical reasons why you can't, instead of even allowing yourself to explore reasons why you can. Often the glass ceiling will kick in without you even noticing what you're doing: you may shut down a thought before it fully consciously enters your brain, or resist the very action that would make something new possible for you.

The aim with this glass ceiling work is to get to a place where you start regularly asking yourself, *is it true that I can't do this thing? Is there another possibility I'm not considering here? Is this really what I want for my life, or just what I think I should want?*

Identifying your unique glass ceiling of possibility is a subtle shift, but it makes such a huge difference when it comes to unleashing the full power of your quiet ambition. Firstly, in listening to yourself, and listening to what you want, and then also by allowing the possibility to grow in your mind that what you want could become real.

It is game-changing as a business owner to be willing – and have the ability – to see things differently. By expanding what we believe might happen, we quite literally expand the possibility of it *actually* playing out in reality.

Uncovering these layers of your identity and noticing your glass ceiling is not a one-time, quick process. Maybe there are some things that you notice first are labels that don't mean anything *to you*. Maybe you'll be able to shed the limits of those labels fairly quickly. Things changed quite fast for me once I realised I was an introvert, for example. Knowing it, and naming it, immediately gave permission for me to own so many things about myself I had previously labelled as "weird".

Something that has taken longer to shift is tying my self-worth to my productivity, and tying my productivity to my success as a human. It crops up again, and again, and again in so many different ways. Every time I see it happening, every time I recognise it, every time it's the same story in a different disguise, I dig deeper into shifting it. I remove a layer of that limitation, and I'm raising my glass ceiling slowly over time.

Digging deeper is not just about understanding the ways in which a story, label or identity is showing up for you. It's about asking yourself how your thoughts and behaviours are matching up to that identity, how that is serving you, and how you can act in alignment with a different story. This is brave and deep work, and something I work with my clients on in our 1:1 coaching sessions, to support them in becoming the fullest expression of themselves.[42]

So many of us find it hard to even listen to, let alone trust and believe in who we really are at our core. We've been taught so much about how we should be, what we should want, that at first it's hard to even recognise that it's not the truth.

Being able to trust in and act upon the desires in our heart – about who we want to be, the impact we want to create, the people we want to reach, the lives we want to live – so much of that comes down to a willingness to do this messy work to unravel the labels, identities and cultural conditioning. Once we can see it, name it, and know that the ceiling exists, we can challenge it. One thought, one belief, one action at a time. Slowly, we build evidence to support a different, more empowering picture of who we are.

This is not about being somebody else. It's about authentically being all that you already are at your core.

---

[42] See https://ruthpoundwhite.com/work-with-me/

I've already written about how our businesses can change the world, and part of the way we do that is in challenging narrow definitions of what's possible for different people. I am personally challenging what it means to be a wife, a mother, to be the breadwinner and *not* the one doing the bulk of the childcare. This dynamic may now be more common than ever before, but it is still hard in the face of generations of beliefs around what it means to be a wife and mother. I constantly have to challenge societal norms, and by doing so I support others in doing the same.

Let's not forget that online business owners are creating a new path. We have the opportunity to create something unique. To work in our own way, to market with personality, to design our businesses in ways that support all of who we are. We get to expand what it means to be an entrepreneur, to be a leader, to be wealthy, to be successful and ambitious.

There are times when our journey and who we are being won't make sense to others. I started a business, ran it for ten years, and then started a different business, eventually selling the first business. I had many concerns about what I did being reckless, and I felt guilty for leaving something successful behind. But the truth is that I knew deep down in my heart, it was what I needed to do. There was a glass ceiling I needed to clear, and I was the only one who could make that decision.

Wherever you are with your business, whether you're making a few tweaks, whether you're figuring out how to make it feel more like your own, or whether you're gearing up for a radical change, remember that everything you have been through, up until now has led you to where you are in the present. Nothing is a waste, nothing is wrong, and nothing is a mistake. It is all part of your journey. And it takes faith to believe that this is true.

I also believe that we all deserve to do fulfilling work, to fully express ourselves and to really *be* ourselves in how we show up. It takes guts to make that choice and to acknowledge that we want more from life. The more we tune into our hearts, the more we ask of life in the name of what's true to us, the more we open up the possibility for others to do, ask for, and get what they want. It is powerful to follow your fulfilment, your joy, your bliss. It's also bloody scary at times.

If you want to dig deeper into how to run a fulfilling business that allows you to be you, if you want to talk about feelings, if you want to claim the desires for the kind of business you want to run, and if you want to figure out how to show up as yourself, stop hiding, and do the thing you want to do, then please get in touch with me. This is my bliss, to support others in their journey to full self-expression through the vehicle of business.

Go to my website ruthpoundwhite.com to find out more and to read the different ways we can work together. For links to everything I do, visit http://ruthpoundwhite.com/everything and for my 1:1 and group coaching packages, visit https://ruthpoundwhite.com/work-with-me/

And remember, keep doing what you're doing because your work really does matter. Not just to you, not just to the people you work with, but to the world.

AFTERWORD

At the time of writing, I've been sitting on this book manuscript for almost a year. Nothing I'm sharing in this book is brand new – both in the sense that others have come before me, and I've personally shared these words on my podcast, in my newsletter and on social media.

And yet, bringing this book to light has been one of the most challenging things I've ever done. I have wondered whether anybody would even read this, and then worried that they would. I have witnessed old wounds that I thought I had healed come right up to the surface again. I have cried (lots).

To see my philosophy laid out so clearly in front of me, to trust in the impact these words get to create and to realise just how much of my business is based on my personal thoughts and ideas has been uncomfortable, powerful, scary and remarkable.

I share this to make it very clear (and in case I didn't say it enough already): being yourself is not comfortable. But there is great beauty to be found in the discomfort. To simultaneously doubt yourself and witness the impact you are already creating.

I have been invited, every single step of the way, to lean deeper into trusting my own process. I am so grateful to everything this experience has taught me, and my biggest wish for you is that you say yes to "the nudge", no matter how uncomfortable that may feel, because incredible things are waiting for you on the other side of that discomfort.

Who am I to put this work into the world? The answer is, who am I not to?

This book is as much for me as it is for you.

One Last Thing…

If you enjoyed this book or found it helpful, I'd be grateful if you could leave a short review on Amazon. Every review makes a difference, helping me to get the "Quietly Ambitious" philosophy in front of more sensitive humans who have important work to do in the world.

Thank you, always, for your support, encouragement and inspiration. I couldn't do this without you.

Ruth x

ACKNOWLEDGEMENTS

This book would not have been possible without the loving support of my friend, mastermind sister and book doula, Genevieve Parker Hill.

Early in 2020, I wrote down an audacious goal on a piece of paper: I was going to write a book within the next 3 years. Then along came Genevieve, promising me that my book was already written. And here we are. Thank you for your encouragement, your vision, your ability to piece together my unique philosophy into a coherent whole (that is so much more powerful than the sum of its parts), and your endless patience while I got my mind on board with this new level of visibility.

Thank you to my coaches and mentors along the way: Jen Carrington, for modelling a deeply intuitive way of doing business; Ray Dodd, for showing me that the world needs more introverts to be visible; Suzy Ashworth, for the inspiration to set my book goal and put this quantum leap into motion; Jamila Theobold, for always holding me radically responsible in the most loving way; Elizabeth Goddard, for always inspiring me to do things my way; Sas Petherick for opening my eyes to everything self-doubt has to teach us.

Thank you to all of my clients for inspiring me with your bravery and willingness to do the work, even when it sometimes feels that nobody is listening. You inspire me to be a better business owner and human with every conversation.

ABOUT THE AUTHOR

Ruth Poundwhite is quietly ambitious — and proud of it! She is a certified coach, feminist marketer and intuitive business mentor who supports highly sensitive humans to scale their businesses without sacrificing who they are. She is particularly passionate about helping women to trust in themselves to build businesses that prioritise both their physical and mental wellbeing. Clients have described the way Ruth works as "nurturing," "kind" and "a breath of fresh air."

As host of the *Quietly Ambitious* podcast, and through her courses and group programs, Ruth has helped thousands of sensitive online business owners radically trust themselves, be more of themselves in their work and offers, increase their bookings, and have their first 5+ figure launches.

Ruth lives by the sea in the South-East of England with her husband and son.

Useful Links

For exclusive bonuses & resources to support you to own your quiet ambition - ruthpoundwhite.com/bookbonus

For a list of everything Ruth does (both free and paid) - https://ruthpoundwhite.com/everything/

For ways to work with me - https://ruthpoundwhite.com/work-with-me/

To subscribe to her newsletter, Letters to Quietly Ambitious Humans - https://ruthpoundwhite.com/newsletter/

To listen to the podcast - https://ruthpoundwhite.com/podcast/

Printed in Great Britain
by Amazon

14081414R00108